Kevin Staffa is a retired Australian commercial lawyer, former soldier and licenced aerobatic pilot. Born in the UK, he grew up in Australia from age five. He has written many as yet unpublished manuscripts reflecting his extensive studies of energy therapy and medicine, physics, cosmology, science, religion and philosophy.

Kevin Staffa

It Must Be True... I Made It Up Myself...!

AUSTIN MACAULEY PUBLISHERS™

LONDON * CAMBRIDGE * NEW YORK * SHARJAH

A CIP catalogue record for this title is available from the British Library.

ISBN 9781398400665 (Paperback)
ISBN 9781398400863 (ePub e-book)

www.austinmacauley.com

First Published 2022
Austin Macauley Publishers Ltd®
1 Canada Square
Canary Wharf
London
E14 5AA

Table of Contents

Chapter 1

What Your Ego Is and Why You Have It...

What You'll Discover in This Chapter...

- Your original ego (your 'ProtoEgo') is ancient and precognitive and it doesn't have wisdom, or even prudence but it does have more recently developed counterparts: your intellectual and religious egos
- Your ego is a part of your psychological apparatus, with the capacity and the tendency to steer your life, like a strong horse that wants to go its own way regardless of where you, the rider, may want to go
- Our egos aren't controlled by our inherited genes
- You can diffuse your ego by using power rather than force – and eventually get beyond even power

Your Ancient Survival Ego... A Run-Away Train...

Your ancient, subconscious survival ego, like mine, is narcissistic, envious, jealous, sulky, petulant, domineering, vindictive, greedy, selfish, judgmental and non-rational. Unless you find and practise ways to dampen your ego, your life will be an uncontrollable roller-coaster; a run-away train.

I'm not advocating that you denounce your ego, that you disown it. I won't ever promote that, because I know it won't work. On the contrary, if the conscious, rational side of you declares war on your survival subconscious ego the conscious rational you will be the loser; you'd become a mental wreck.

You can't evolve into a more effective, more successful version of yourself by condemning your subconscious survival ego. After all, it's a big part of who you are and you can't, at one and the same time, condemn yourself and grow into something better.

Use Your Heart to Forgive Your Ego...

Your ego, your psyche, is the outward expression of your subconscious perception of sensory data from the outside world. You screen all your sensory data inputs through filters that you subconsciously enforce by your ego. What is allowed through your filters creates your reality.

However, you, like me, have something that is potentially far more powerful than your ego, and that is your heart. Whereas your ego has no compassion, no concept of forgiveness, your heart has innate wisdom and knows compassion, empathy and forgiveness. The starting point to defusing your ego is to forgive yourself for being a victim of your ego and to forgive your ego for making you its victim. By doing this you will permit yourself to evolve beyond who you currently are.

Use Ego-Less Power, Not Ego-Full Force...

In later chapters of this book, I will delve into the concepts of power and force. In doing so, I'll refer to the Map of Consciousness (MoC) devised by David R. Hawkins MD, PhD (1927-2012).

I don't fully endorse or agree with everything David Hawkins wrote and taught; as will become apparent in later chapters of this book – but I do believe there is a great deal of helpful material that emerged as a result of his extensive clinical work on kinesiology. But for now let's find out more about you and your enigmatic ego.

What You Want to Achieve in Life...

There are things that we all aspire to, but few of us consistently achieve. For example, most of us would say we want to:

- Rid ourselves of fear, anxiety and stress – to stop worrying about everything from the economy, our retirement, our health, that cortisol-filled belly fat we can't get rid of, our finances, our children, and so on
- Have a healthier lifestyle
- Have positive, constructive, enjoyable relationships with our partners, children, families, in-laws, work colleagues and others
- Feel spiritually whole and at peace with ourselves
- Be free from debt

- Be free from negative behaviours
- Be free from self-sabotage

The aspirations I've just listed above are your conscious mind's aspirations, not those of your subconscious, ancient ego.

Your ego doesn't really look to the future as your conscious mind understands that concept. Instead, your ego projects the past into your present and into your future by having outmoded signature behavioural loops that it rigidly follows, for good or for bad – and it's often for bad.

So, your subconscious ego is in your way if you're failing to consistently achieve any of the above, or if you seem to sabotage yourself.

Your Ego Is Solipsistic...

Solipsism is actually a conscious (not sub-conscious) intellectual (that is a cognitive, frontal lobe) 'belief' that it's only each person's subjective perceptions that create each person's version of reality.

This is more-or-less paraphrasing what I say, above, about your ego being a subconscious run-away train that's shackled by its myopic filtering systems and signature behavioural loops.

The difference is that the fact that we have conscious solipsism shows us that your ego operates not only subconsciously but that it also infiltrates, eavesdrops on and vetoes your conscious thoughts. So, your subconscious ego is a big deal; and this realisation leads to the question: which part of you, your subconscious or your conscious, is having your thoughts and making your decisions?

What are Thoughts...?

Your ego can be equated to your 'mind', but it's probably more apt to see it as the source of, and the process of, filtering information and making decisions; which really means it's 'thinking' on a subconscious level. At the same time, your ego is eavesdropping on and vetoing 'decisions' or ideas of your conscious frontal lobe that your ego doesn't like.

This is an important point because it's often been said, rightly or wrongly, that 'energy follows thought' or 'that which is held to mind tends to materialise' for you, the thinker of the thought. So, by your ego obstructing decisions your conscious frontal lobe would choose to make it's sabotaging who you can be or become. Your ego does this in the misguided belief that it's protecting you; that it's thereby ensuring your 'survival'.

Research tells us that the time lapse between an internally sensed stimulus until it is filtered (by your subconscious, signature sensory input filters or biases) is a mere $1/10,000^{th}$ of a second, or $1/10^{th}$ of a millisecond. That's how quickly your ego seizes control of your thought processes and imposes a decision on you that results in your next act or omission.

However, once you consciously realise that this is going on, you can gently start to wrest control for sensory and data collection and filtering, and decision making, from your ego and use your conscious reason and response to replace blind reaction or subconscious editing or censorship by your ego.

The Ego as Guardian... And Enforcer of Habits...

The ego is overseer of much of our subconscious mind processes, which is a massive data base of stored programs that filter environmental signals and react with hardwired signature behavioural reactions (that is, habitual reactions) without questioning whether there might be a better way. The subconscious mind is like a hugely powerful programmable hard drive.

What's Happening When We 'Think'...?

We all think, but trying to break down the elements that make up thought is challenging. Thoughts can be looked at, correctly, as biological or physiological phenomena; and in a moment I will look at how our individual bodily cells constantly 'think' and make decisions, without us even being aware of it, and that tells us that most of our thoughts occur beyond our consciousness.

Therefore, we can say that some thoughts, such as at the non-cerebral cellular level, are subconscious and others, at the cerebral level, may be or may not be conscious; which means thoughts may be able to be distinguished as either consciously aware thoughts or as consciously unaware (that is, as subconscious) thoughts.

What we do know is that every cerebral thought is the result of electrical signals passing through a network of the brain's approximately 86 billion neurons; but that doesn't explain what thoughts are.

Even neuroscientists can't tell you anything more than the term 'thought' is simply an ambiguous concept that encompasses numerous different cognitive processes that rely on our biology as the underlying hardware.

Thoughts and Brainwaves...

According to current neuroscience, our prefrontal cortex helps organise thought processes; which would suggest that our conscious mind not only has our thoughts but also *makes our decisions*; but that doesn't account for our behind-the-scenes ego which appears to act as the puppet master when it comes to governing our life.

If we look deeper, as neuroscience has already done, we come across the role of brainwaves; which are currently described as ripples of neural activity oscillating at different frequencies across the brain. However, brainwaves of themselves don't appear to be capable of reining in our all-powerful ego. It's likely that one of the subconscious signature input filtering loops under the control of our ego actually determines what brainwave frequencies predominate in our brains at any given moment in time. So, perhaps our brain hardware is also under the thumb of our ego.

How Many Egos do we Have...?

Our ancient survival ego, emerged before our frontal cortex developed and is undoubtedly the most powerful manifestation of ego that we have. Its job is to make sure we survive.

It's our original or ancestral manifestation of our ego; so I may refer to it as our ProtoEgo, meaning source ego or earliest form ego; the word 'proto' from the ancient Greek, meaning 'earliest form of' or 'source', 'ancestral' and 'original'.

Our ego also manifests in other guises; and I'm primarily interested in the intellectual ego and the religious ego. So, we'll be looking at them.

Our Original Ego... Our ProtoEgo... And Physical Survival...

It's our ProtoEgo that's inherently selfish, greedy, narcissistic, fearful, unfeeling of others, and totally self-absorbed. In ancient times it was these qualities that made our ProtoEgo our physical saviour in a hostile world of equally ProtoEgo-driven selfish, greedy individuals who also hadn't developed the skills of co-operation on large group levels.

It was the emergence of our mammalian brain, our limbic system, that gave us the capacity for higher emotions, such as sympathy, empathy and love that enabled our ProtoEgo to see that our survival might be enhanced if we lived within cooperative groups, starting with our immediate family group; but that still hasn't changed our ProtoEgo from being selfish, grasping, self-pitying, envious, self-centred, vengeful, and so on.

ProtoEgo Encounters Frontal Lobe...

The biggest challenge to our ProtoEgo has come from the emergence of our rational frontal lobe, by which we can see that some of the ProtoEgo's beliefs, biases and behaviours are counterproductive. The ProtoEgo's reaction to this 'threat' has been to eavesdrop on and sabotage any frontal lobe thoughts that it believes jeopardise our 'safety'.

The problem for us is that to the ProtoEgo anything that is unfamiliar, such as a change in our habitual behaviour (such as, say, giving up smoking, giving up drinking too much, or giving up our extravagant lifestyle habits) is seen as a threat to our survival. So, it keeps to its unhelpful signature filtering and behavioural loops, taking you along for the ride.

This unhelpful, habitual ego-driven behaviour is what needs to be changed for you to become a successful person in whatever aspect of your life that isn't giving you the most beneficial outcomes.

Cells and 'Thought'... And Cells and Awareness...

Each of us has a physical body made up of about 70 trillion single cells, each one of which has 'awareness' of its micro-environment; and it's their responses to micro-environmental signals that steer our lives; and your conscious mind can never be in control of that cellular process.

Insight: Your life's journey isn't controlled by your inherited genes. Rather, it's controlled by how your individual cells respond to their micro-environment and thereby direct their physiology, and thereby dictate your physiological behaviour at the cellular level.

According to Bruce H. Lipton, Ph.D., cell biologist, author of *The Biology of Belief* (Hay House Inc., 2008), and Professor at Stanford University School of Medicine, the central driver of your behaviour and your fate is your perception of and reaction to, or response to, your environment. Lipton says that scientific research shows that this control comes from 'above the genes' in other words it's 'epigenetic'.

Insight: Epigenetics is the science of how environmental signals select, modify and regulate gene activity.

It's Not Genetics That Drives Your Ego... Or Your Life Outcomes...

What this means is that your ego (mind) does not act the way it does because of your genes. Your ego is not DNA driven.

The Other Egos... Intellectual and Religious...

So, you're not a loser because you inherited loser genes. You're a loser because you're permitting yourself to be, or choosing to be, a loser by letting your ego control your life, as we shall see. You've got only yourself to blame; which means you can change things; you can empower yourself and enrich your life, and become a winner. So, you have to recognise that you also have ego intellect and a religious ego.

Insight: What Bruce Lipton realised, and what he says in *The Biology of Belief,* is that Charles Darwin got it wrong when he suggested (as he did in his book *The Origin of The Species*, 1859) that 'hereditary factors' passed from parent to child *control* the characteristics and outcomes of an individual's life.

It's Not About Darwinian Evolution... It's About Awareness...

In actual fact, the human evolution narrative isn't even of Darwin's invention. The first scientist to posit that human biological evolution appeared to be an unguided occurrence was the Frenchman, Jean-Baptiste de Lamarck; and he did so a full 50 years before Darwin popped up.

What's more, modern science is now suggesting that Lamarck's theory, which puts forward a much less brutal position than that of Darwin, is far closer to reality; because Lamarck suggested that 'evolution' was based on an 'instructive', co-operative interaction between organisms and their environment; meaning the Lamarck's theory of 'evolution' is based on awareness and choice; unlike Darwin's which is based on genetic determinism, or fate.

Insight: It's now patently clear to enlightened scientists – but will never be clear to the die-hards such as Richard Dawkins and Sam Harris – that the Darwinian concept of spontaneous, non-divine biological origin and evolution of mankind is flawed; just plain wrong; but more on that theory of ego intellect, later.

Darwin Is Wrong Because Our Cells Are 'Intelligent...'

As Lipton points out (p7 of *The Biology of Belief*) each nucleus-containing cell of our bodies (they're called eukaryotes if they contain a nucleus) possesses the functional equivalent of our body's nervous system, excretory system, endocrine system, muscle and skeletal systems, circulatory system, integument (skin) system, reproductive system and immune system.

Scientists have already shown that these eukaryotes can survive on their own; which proves that each nucleus-containing cell of your body has intent and purpose, or 'awareness'.

These cells are smart enough to try to actively seek environments that support their survival and to try to avoid hostile or toxic environments. Each of them does this by analysing thousands of stimuli from their micro-environment and by then choosing appropriate behavioural responses to enhance the chances of their individual survival. In other words, they are not the victims of your DNA.

These cells have cellular memory which enables them to pass on what they've learned to their successors. The classic example of this is when we develop antibodies to diseases, such as measles, and subsequently created cells of our body 'remember' what their predecessors learned.

The Problem Is Your Ego and the Ego-Environment it Creates, Not Your Body or Your Genes...

When we get far enough above the cellular view, and genetic view, of our bodies we can look at the mind (our ProtoEgo and our intellectual and religious ego) and the signature behavioural programmes it employs. This is worthwhile because those programmes (our signature or default behavioural programmes or signature or default decisions making biases) are as much our environment as what we see around us in the external world.

As Bruce Lipton observes in *The Biology of Belief* (p19), when cellular biologists like him are studying cultured cells and see that they are ailing they look first to the cell's environment, not the cell itself, for the cause.

By analogy, if your life is off the rails in some respect, you should look first not at your genes (not your DNA) but to your ego's default filtering and behavioural programmes; you should look at your ego-environment. That's where you'll likely find the answers. This means looking at your ProtoEgo, ego intellect and religious ego.

What you Learned in This Chapter...

- Genetic determination is a myth, which means you are not a victim of fate; something else is driving your life's outcomes on all levels
- Your subconscious mind (your ego) operates according to embedded signature filtering and behavioural programmes and those programmes are not genetic, and they can be changed
- There are three key manifestations of your ego I'm interested in: your ProtoEgo (that is, your ancestral survival ego), your intellectual ego and your religious ego

Chapter 2

Your Brain and Your Ego... and Your Heart...

What You'll Discover in This Chapter...

- There are 3 key parts of your brain, and understanding their origins and role will help you understand how it is your ego bosses you around
- Your conscious frontal lobe is the most recent part of the human brain to develop, but it only operates in short bursts, and it isn't guiding your life's outcomes – but your heart works full time
- To succeed consistently at life, you need to pacify your subconscious mind, your ego
- Your ego's goals are not your frontal lobe's goals and not your heart's goals
- Leaving aside agape love, which I'll look at in Chapter 12, 'emotional intelligence' is a myth, and I'm not convinced that agape love is an emotion

Mind the Ego Gap...

The reason you may consistently fail at some or all of your conscious goals is that they are not your ego's goals. There's a gap between your conscious mind and ego giant within you. Unless you learn how to transform your ego from being an enigma and antagonist to being your conscious brain's ally (and your heart's ally) you will forever struggle in all those areas where you are not satisfied with your life.

'Brain' V Subconscious 'Mind' (Ego) V 'Consciousness...'

Your brain and your subconscious mind (ego) aren't the same thing. 'Mind' refers to the functions of the brain, what it does. Your mind operates on both the subconscious (ego) level and the conscious (frontal lobe) level. The 'brain' is the biological organ, the biological hardware, that enables those functions to happen. If you're failing, then you have to address both your brain architecture and your brain function, and you can.

Your Heart Has a Key Role... If You Let it...

Interestingly, neuroscientists now believe that mindfulness occurs not only in our brain but also in our heart and our gut, but for now we're going to focus on what's happening inside your head, with your ego.

What Your Subconscious Brain and Mind Do...

Your subconscious brain and mind have five main functions that I'm interested in:

- First, your subconscious brain communicates with the rest of your body via high-speed neurotransmitters without you being aware of it and your subconscious mind is privy to this – and that means that it, not your conscious mind, is in control of your body
- Secondly, your subconscious mind decides when to deploy hormones (chemicals) into your blood system, which of them to deploy, and how often to deploy them
- Thirdly, your subconscious controls your autonomous nervous system
- Fourthly, your subconscious, by your ego, has its own agenda, a 'survival' agenda, and it doesn't want your conscious mind to interfere, let alone override, its 'survival' decisions, no matter how whacky and harmful those decisions may be
- Fifthly, you subconscious mind (ego) makes all your important decisions – yes, all of them

Hormones... Your Inner Chemical Arsenal...

Unlike a neural signal, the deployment of hormones in your body isn't instantaneous or transient. Hormones are constantly and repeatedly secreted at the instigation of your subconscious mind; and these hormones can remain in your body for a long period, continuing to have effects on your physiology, your well-being and your conscious state of mind.

Some hormones (such as cortisol, norepinephrine and adrenaline) can be thought of as 'stress hormones'. If there are repeated releases of stress hormones into your body, over prolonged periods, they can build up and get to toxic levels. You'll end up being unwell because they result in the impairment of your immune system.

Insight: Most mature males have belly fat that's full of an accumulated, harmful hormone: cortisol.

Insight: This is important. It's your subconscious mind (your ego) that's in control of the arsenal of stress hormones in your body. It's your subconscious that decides whether or not to pump these stress hormones into your system. Without any input from your conscious mind, your subconscious (your ego) decides if, when and which hormones will be secreted and how often.

Your Brain... The Three-Part (or Triune) Brain Model...

In this model of the brain's architecture the original part of the human brain to develop contains basic survival neurological hardware. This survival brain has only simple emotions (more 'feelings' than emotions); such as fear, lust, anger, curiosity and anxiety. It's not self-aware. Its awareness is sensory.

The second part of the human brain developed long after the original survival brain. It's often referred to as the 'mammalian' brain or the 'limbic' system, but I may refer to it as the emotional brain. It enables you to express more advanced feelings; such as love, compassion, sorrow, pity for others (rather than just self-pity), and so on. Like the survival brain the emotional brain is not self-aware. Love, however, is a very tricky emotion because of your ego; so I look up close at your ego and love in Chapter 12.

The third and last part of the human brain to develop was the neocortex. It's made up of the primate brain and the frontal lobe. I may refer to this as the conscious brain. The frontal lobe is self-aware and enables you to behave cognitively (that is, consciously, thoughtfully). Unlike the survival brain and the emotional brain, the frontal lobe is capable of 'reason' and can apply 'logic' but it has been infiltrated by your ego, and that's a big problem.

Explaining the human brain in this triune, or three-part, way was probably one of the biggest leaps forward in understanding what makes us tick. It was devised by Paul MacLean, M.D., who was director of the Laboratory of Brain Evolution and Behaviour of the National Institute of Mental Health, in the USA, between 1971 and 1985.

So, with MacLean's help we've now de-mystified your brain hardware by showing that it can be described as having three quite distinct yet closely connected parts:

- First, the non-thinking original survival brain, what MacLean called the 'Reptilian' brain or 'R-complex'.
- Second, the non-thinking mammalian brain, the home of higher emotions – enabling you to have advanced emotions (such as love, empathy, joy and sadness), and more complex and co-operative social behaviours
- Third, the neocortex, which is made up of the non-rational primate brain and the rational thinking frontal lobe – it's the frontal lobe (but not the primate brain) that gives you your capacity for thinking, analysis, logic, contemplation, a greater ability to co-operate with others, problem solving ability, innovation and self-awareness

Another Brain Model… The Two Aspects Brain Model…

The second brain model I'm interested in is one that researchers such as neurologist Richard Restak use. It describes the brain as having two aspects:

- One aspect is described as being automatic and reactive (not responsive, only reactive) – being the equivalent of the survival and emotional parts in MacLean's triune brain model
- The other aspect is described as being controlling and reflective, referring only to the frontal lobe

Both these brain models are a good place to start our journey into unravelling your ego's weaknesses and failings. Importantly, what you have to remember, if you're going to go beyond being an ego serf is:

- It's your subconscious mind (ego), not your conscious mind, that's, misguidedly, giving you your bad results in life, and it does it to try to keep you alive – it's your survival mind

- It's also your subconscious mind, not your conscious mind, that's making the bad life decisions that are keeping you where you are
- Your subconscious (survival) mind/ego and your conscious mind both have what can be called 'intuition' but it's your subconscious intuition that prevails for many aspects of modern life
- There's a world of difference between *sensory* awareness and *sensory* intuition (which your subconscious survival mind/ego has) and *self-* awareness and *cognitive* intuition (which your subconscious survival mind/ego doesn't have and your frontal lobe does have)

Emotions and So-Called 'Emotional Intelligence'

Your subconscious mind (ego) can't think. It's governed by how it 'feels'. It reacts because it can't respond. Response requires thought, analysis, weighing options; which your subconscious mind (your ego) is incapable of, which is why it often makes bad decisions for you.

When it comes to emotions, things can get confusing because some commentators describe what they call 'emotional intelligence' ('EI'); which they promote as a means of 'recognising' your emotions (that is, your feelings) and those of others, and using this recognition 'skill' to guide and improve your *thinking* and *behaviour*.

You will realise that this view of emotional intelligence is dubious once you understand that it's invariably your subconscious mind (ego) that makes you subject to your emotions; and that it does so by using embedded automatic reactions to deploy certain, specific, hormones that trigger those feelings, or emotions, without your conscious mind having a say in it.

Subconscious gut instincts, or subconscious feelings, come from your non-thinking, pre-cognitive survival mind (your ego). Nonetheless, if you buy a book on EI it will likely tell you that by developing (that is, by changing) your EI you will thereby:

- Know yourself
- Control your emotions
- Develop empathy with the feelings of others – which presumably includes others who don't yet have EI

- Use social skills in an effective way – which presumably means even with people who don't reciprocate because they don't yet have EI
- Such EI proponents will suggest that developing your EI involves:
- 'Mindfulness' – being *self*-aware and understanding of yourself and others
- Being in control of your own thoughts, emotions and needs
- Being positive and self-motivated
- Using empathy – being able to put yourself in other people's shoes
- Communicating effectively
- Using emotional *reasoning*

The problem with this conventional EI approach is it doesn't address the fundamental dichotomy between:

- On the one hand, your *sensory* aware, but not *self*-aware, subconscious mind (ego), which is the home of your emotions and is a high-speed decision-maker that controls a specific arsenal of hormones which it uses for 'survival', by bullying you to do things its way; making you literally feel sick if you don't do things its way
- On the other hand, your *self*-aware frontal lobe, which doesn't control this hormonal arsenal, is a slow thinker and operates only 3% to 5% of the time

Unless you address the fundamental communication issue between your conscious and your ego, and unless you embed new filters (or biases or defaults, if you prefer) into your subconscious, then emotional intelligence is just a concept devised by someone's frontal lobe that's totally ignored by your ego and theirs.

It's all about the difference between trying to force yourself (that is, trying to force your ego) to change and enabling yourself (that is, enabling your ego) to change, by giving your subconscious mind new filters for the information it receives.

Insight: To me, the concept of acquiring emotional intelligence sounds like trying to force your subconscious emotions or decisions to be filtered through your frontal lobe, and to my frontal lobe that sounds dubious.

On the other hand, enabling your subconscious (that is, your ego) to react differently by giving it different defaults or biases is a different matter altogether. If you do that, you're making emotions potentially 'intelligent', you're making your ego potentially, vicariously, intelligent; but in my belief that can only be achieved through the heart, as I will endeavour to show.

WIsdom Verses Emotional Intelligence Versus Intelligent Emotions...

Subconscious emotions, and reactions, are not based on understanding or on learning from experience.

Subconscious emotions are about your ego blindly reacting to sensory inputs in the same way, over and over, even when it's not good for you to do so.

Wisdom is the opposite of blinkered subconscious ego-driven emotion because wisdom comes from the conscious mind, from the heart.

Wisdom isn't about blindly reacting to circumstances you encounter but about learning to do things better, to get a better outcome.

Wisdom is about *responding* rather than *reacting* to life's challenges. Unless you couple your raw, subconscious ego emotions to frontal lobe thought and then *respond*, rather than *react*, you can never have 'intelligent' emotions.

Emotions or feelings work like this...

1) You have a subconsciously or consciously perceived 'survival threat' (e.g., you've just been told you're fired) – and your ego kicks in	2) The ego alarm causes an instantaneous subconscious hormone release (e.g., cortisol, adrenalin, norepinephrine)	3) The hormone release creates a negative 'feeling', a negative emotion – which is what the ego wants

⇨	4) The hormone release triggers an emotional 'survival' 'reaction' (e.g., anger, fear, panic, anxiety)	⇨	5) In this state you – your ego – then makes your next decision and directs your next action

There's no 'intelligence', no frontal lobe involvement, in how emotions arise. They emerge as a reaction to a stimulus or circumstance which can be sensory, experiential or just imagined. The only exception is when the heart gets involved; as in the case of agape love, which I'll deal with in Chapter 12 of this book.

An Overview of the Brain Hardware at Your Ego's Disposal in Habitual Subconscious (Ego-Driven) Behaviour...

Your *amygdala* is the source of your feelings of fear and physically unpleasant sensations, such as accelerated heartbeat, shortness of breath, hyperventilation and sweating. It decides you should feel afraid and so it causes a physiological reaction, to get your attention – to ensure you survive.

Your *insula* causes your gut responses, such as alarm, dread, panic and despair.

Working closely with your amygdala and insula is your *anterior cingulate*. When it's triggered, you'll immediately (in about 1/10,000th of a second) sense that something's wrong.

These three brain areas are the worry centres of your subconscious brain. They operate like pickets (outer early warning observers), sentries (closer in warning observers) and bodyguards (last line of defence).

When these areas of your brain activate your *basal ganglia* also go active. It's your basal ganglia that are responsible for your *automatic*, *non-cognitive* thoughts and actions; your physical and subconscious reactions (or habitual behaviours).

Your basal ganglia are made up of your *caudate* (responsible for automatic conclusions or interpretations – which may be right or wrong – from sensory input) and your *putamen* (responsible for your automatic reactions – which may cause you more harm than good).

Insight: Your basal ganglia can be thought of as the habit centre of your brain responsible for your rote (that is, pre-cognitive) behaviour. If you've got any bad habits or behaviours your basal ganglia are involved.

Your basal ganglia are involved every time your subconscious mind (ego) interprets sensations as uncomfortable or unwelcome; even if they're merely unfamiliar rather than dangerous or harmful. It will then decide what you do next, before your conscious brain is even aware of what's going on. It will use one or more of its embedded signature filtering and behavioural programmes or loops to decide and act.

So, we now know what brain hardware is involved with your ego when you do something pre-cognitively and habitually in response to a sensation, experience or circumstance that your subconscious survival mind (ego) decides it doesn't like; regardless of whether that sensation, experience or circumstance might actually improve your situation if you allow it to run its course.

Insight: Throughout this process of habitual behaviour your cognitive frontal cortex is a passive bystander.

Insight: Every time your ego mind engages in this knee-jerk reaction to these types of 'uncomfortable' or unfamiliar sensations or circumstances it reinforces the embedded neurological 'wiring' in your subconscious brain making the habit even harder to break; which is why we say, "You can't teach an old dog new tricks," thereby fostering and reinforcing the false belief that we can't change.

That old saying is wrong. You can teach an old dog (your ego) new tricks. You can change, as we shall see.

'Intervention' Is the Key to Breaking the Ego's Destructive Cycle...

The only way to break this destructive, automatic ego-driven cycle is to consciously intervene before the action stage, or earlier; with frontal lobe thought or analysis; or, better still, with the innate consciousness and conscience of your heart. The aim of the intervention is to make raw, dull emotions become intelligent emotions. If you want an insight, now, into the difference between raw and intelligent emotions you could skip forward to Chapter 12, which looks at how your ego sees love, and what love really is.

Intervention Requires Egoless Attention...

Your ability to attend consciously to something or to consciously focus on it, is an extraordinarily powerful, if underutilised, ability. It can be far more powerful than your ego's rigid 'survival' focused paranoia and arsenal of stress hormones. Learning to consciously focus can literally change your life.

Insight: It's been scientifically demonstrated, time and again, that what you consciously focus on is who you *are* at that time and who you can *become*.

Your Frontal Lobe Is Asleep...!

According to neuroscientists (that is, brain scientists) we're only conscious (that is, self-aware) between about 3% and 5% of the time. For the rest of the time, even when we are awake, our frontal lobe is actually snoozing.

Insight: This neuro-science ignores the fact that your heart is conscious all the time; but let's put that thought to one side for now.

To put it another way, your logical frontal lobe generally only has input into what you're doing about 3% to 5% of the time; it's been scientifically proven, and you're no exception; and guess who's in charge for the other 97% of the time: your ego.

Insight: You can check whether your conscious brain is switched on by asking yourself, "Am I conscious?" This will instantly switch on your frontal lobe; but you have to keep doing it, because you'll quickly switch off again, without you even noticing.

Insight: If you can learn something, even if you have to initially learn it logically using your frontal lobe, such as a language, the piano, unusual bodily movement (as in dance steps, gymnastics or martial arts), sculpture and the like, you will master it far more deeply, you will learn to do it automatically, if you can embed that programme into your subconscious brain; but there are some things you can only learn with your heart.

The Three Agendas in Your Head...

Your three-part mind (subconscious ego survival mind, subconscious ego emotional mind and conscious rational brain) operates like 3 interconnected biological computers, each of which has its own:

- Sense of reality
- Priorities
- Memory
- Agenda

The 'ProtoBrain' or 'Hindbrain'...

From time to time, I may refer to the two subconscious parts of the brain (the original survival brain and the emotional brain) as the 'ProtoBrain' or the 'HindBrain', instead of the subconscious brain or the survival brain. All three terms mean the same thing for the purposes of this book.

The reason I'll sometimes use the term ProtoBrain is because the word 'proto' is ancient Greek for 'earliest form of', 'ancestral' or ancient and I want to emphasise the point that those two subconscious parts of the brain are *ancient* in comparison to your modern logical, conscious brain. For hundreds of millennia, they've been in charge of what your ancestors – and you – do and what you can achieve, *and they're still in charge* through your ego mind.

Insight: It's thought by mainstream science that human-like predecessors of today's humans were able to survive for hundreds of thousands, if not millions, of years in sole reliance on a ProtoBrain structure and ego mind. We still have the same brain hardware and it's been very good at doing its job of keeping us alive; and they've got no intention of giving up that role to your conscious frontal lobe – that will never happen; but they can be quelled by your heart.

Subconscious Survival Software Programmes...

It's been the job of our ProtoBrain and ProtoEgo to ensure that we survive. To do this, they long ago developed their own rigid pre-cognitive survival programmes (like software programmes in a computer).

Forward... To the Past...

But those pre-cognitive programmes were not designed for your modern, cognitive, 21st century life – and therein lies a huge problem, as we shall see. The primary functions of your ProtoBrain and ProtoEgo are your self-preservation. They 'think' only in terms of 'survival', and they're:

- Paranoid
- Habitual
- Impulsive
- Obsessive
- Rigid

This is you, your subconscious brain, your ego-mind that we're talking about. It's mine, too.

Your ProtoBrain and ProtoEgo Carry Out Surveillance... They Eavesdrop...

You will *always* have this original ProtoBrain/ProtoEgo tag-team because without them you would die. The ProtoBrain will *always* be rigid, obsessive, impulsive, habitual and paranoid; and will always eavesdrop on your conscious brain, and has the power to veto decisions your conscious brain might want to make. And that's a perfect system as far as your ProtoEgo is concerned. However, your ProtoEgo can be quelled by your heart.

ProtoBrain and ProtoEgo Aren't the Same...

Your ProtoBrain is the ancestral brain hardware that must operate 24/7 or your body would cease to function and you would die. Your ProtoEgo is like an ancient body guard that never sleeps and will try to get your ProtoBrain to send alerts or other signals to your body.

Insight: This capacity of your ProtoBrain and ProtoEgo to eavesdrop on your conscious brain and to veto conscious decisions explains why it's so hard, for example, to give up habits such as smoking, alcohol or other drugs; and why it's often so difficult for some people to lose discretionary weight or break bad habits such as being a consumer junkie.

Your ProtoBrain and ProtoEgo are Addicts...

One of the significant characteristics of your ProtoBrain and ProtoEgo is that they addictively repeat the same decision-making patterns (reaction patterns) over and over, oblivious to learning better ways to deal with the evolving 'survival' challenges of 21st century life. They're using the same pre-cognitive reactions to today's 'survival' issues (which come largely from a cognitive world environment) as those they developed in the pre-stone age.

Your ProtoBrain Is Mechanical...

Your survival brain has been referred to as 'mechanical' because of its propensity to operate as if it's running up and down a railway line without any willingness to change direction; without the ability to decide on a different way of reacting to things. It has a rigid, narrow world view, expressed through your ProtoEgo, and it sees no reason to change that world view no matter how much your conscious brain might disagree with it.

Insight: Consciously disagreeing with your ProtoBrain or ProtoEgo isn't enough for you to change your results in life.

Insight: Despite the development of our subconscious emotional brain and our conscious modern brain our ProtoBrain still controls our muscles, balance, autonomic functions (such as breathing and heartbeat) and our entire autonomic nervous systems. Without our ProtoBrain in charge of these functions we'd be dead.

Your ProtoBrain Is a Feeler not a Thinker...

It's your modern, conscious brain, not your ProtoBrain, that uses language and logic; notwithstanding that your language ability is actually embedded in your subconscious, making it 'automatic'. This explains why people often speak before they think. Your subconscious ego brain gets along quite happily without logic or reason. The subconscious ego brain has always blissfully operated on the basis of how it 'feels' without the need to 'think', and it always will.

Insight: Given that your ProtoBrain's language, and your ProtoEgo's language, is 'feelings' then to bridge the gap between your conscious and your subconscious may require you to try to implant the feelings you want into our subconscious to get it to do things it wouldn't otherwise do; instead of trying to use reason or logic to persuade it to change.

Most of your daily behaviour is subconscious and habitual – and that's a good thing for such things as driving your car as it frees up your conscious mind to perform conscious tasks.

But there are a lot of negative behaviours that may be part of your routine behaviour – such as pigging out on snacks whenever you watch TV, having a cigarette when you have a glass of wine, snapping at people who disagree with you, wasting your hard-earned money on consumer rubbish or just wasting your time on mindless pursuits.

Insight: Your brain is 'neuroplastic' meaning that it can be re-wired so that it programmes new habitual behaviours that might make you more successful in your daily life – and it can respond to your heart – and that's how your ego can be overcome.

Rote Biases are Dangerous and Obstructive...

Many of your subconscious, reactive behaviours are nothing more than irrational biases that are embedded in the neuronal connections in your brain. Some of them are essential to keep you alive.

However, your ProtoBrain, and your ProtoEgo now have a far greater catchment area of what they consider 'survival' issues (or what I might refer to as 'ProtoStressors'). The result is that their reactive, knee-jerk, snap decision-making cause you all manner of problems on a daily basis in your modern life.

In the table below is a brief but telling comparison of how your conscious and subconscious minds operate differently.

Insight: This table doesn't refer to your heart.

Conscious Mind	Subconscious Mind
Thoughtful analysis	Mindless habits
Cognitive curiosity, empowerment	Sensory curiosity, sameness
Strategic thinking	Unbridled emotional reaction, keeper of your inner chemical arsenal (hormones)
Inventive	Information filtering biases
Considered judgments and conclusions	Limited or no programmes to deal with modern life's daily issues
Aspirational – doesn't want to be held back	Not aspirational – a blind enforcer of your comfort zone limits, doesn't like change
Open-minded, intellectually empowering	Paranoid, suspicious
Flexible	Rigid

What...! More Egos...! Ego Mirror Neurons and Ego Peer Biases...

Many of us reinforce these negative ego-driven behavioural patterns, or biases, by aligning ourselves to peer groups (which are more accurately described as 'influencer' groups) that reinforce what we're doing, but more on that later.

What You Learned in This Chapter...

- You don't need emotional intelligence, instead you need intelligent emotions, and they're likely to come from your heart rather than your frontal lobe

- Your logical mind is actually asleep for at least 95% of the time, which means that your subconscious brain and ego are in control for most of your life. This means your future is in their hands unless you intervene – and your heart doesn't sleep

- The subconscious brain and ego are in charge of a very special arsenal of hormones that they can release, which gives them the power to cause you to react the way those hormones are intended to make you react. For example, if your subconscious brain triggers the release of adrenalin, you'll be on high alert. Your subconscious uses this chemical arsenal to bully you into doing things its way, but you can use your heart to sidestep this

- People are at their most powerful, and achieve the most when they develop a skill to the point that their subconscious brain does it 'automatically' (that is, without conscious input), putting them in a state of mental flow or 'genius'. That's a good thing with skills such as driving a motor vehicle, riding a bicycle, doing exercise or going about your daily functions such as eating; but it can be taken much further – to the point where you can develop new subconscious mind programmes to overcome weaknesses in all areas of your life, as we shall see

- You can change who you are and what you get out of life – and you can use your frontal lobe, and better still your heart, to achieve this

Chapter 3
Ego Alchemy and Ego Feelings...

What You'll Discover in This Chapter...

- You can't live without it and it's tough living with it – your enigmatic survival ego is a nuisance as well as a necessity.
- How you're ruled and fooled by your subconscious ego mind, a sneaky alchemist with an arsenal of special hormones.
- All those feelings you have... whose feelings are they anyway?
- It's not easy to get behind your ego mind's super firewalled security measures.
- You're spirally dynamic.

The Alchemist... And Hormones...

Your survival brain (ProtoBrain) is driven by feelings, created by hormones (chemicals), which it deploys without any conscious input from you, without you having any choice in the matter. It's nature's greatest alchemist.

What Are Hormones...?

When you think that you've got, say, 70 trillion or more cells in your body you would wonder how it is they manage to function as a unit. Imagine trying to get just the earth's population (less than 8 billion as at 2020) to co-operate; a feat beyond comprehension. Yet your body achieves co-operation on a level that science cannot fathom.

Your body carries out millions of operations every second of every hour of every day for your entire life; and its secret catalysts to trigger these operations are hormones.

Insight: The word 'hormone' comes from the ancient Greek *hormone*, meaning 'to set in motion'.

Hormones are tiny chemical messengers that move continuously through your bloodstream. Once they reach their target cells, these hormones bind onto the cell's surface receptors where they stimulate a specific activity.

Hormones play essential roles in every aspect of your daily life, including growth, reproduction, metabolic function and mood.

All of our hormones are vital for our existence, but some of them are looked on as superstars such as:

Melatonin	The biological clock hormone, responsible for how alert you feel through the day. If you feel drowsy, it has to do with melatonin.
Serotonin	Which is involved with mood, appetite and sleep cycles, and with PMS and moody teenagers.
Thyroxin	A metabolic rate accelerator and protein synthesiser used by cells to build protein.
Epinephrine or Adrenalin(e)	Responsible for the 'fight or flight' reaction – when it's deployed, it will result in dilated pupils, increased heart rate and muscle tensing.
Norepinephrine or Noradrenalin(e)	Controls heart and blood pressure and plays a role in sleep, arousal and emotions. Too much will make you feel anxious and too little will make you feel sedated or even depressed.
Dopamine	Controls heart rate and assists in perception, with deciphering, what's 'real' and what isn't.
Ghrelin	A hunger stimulant, that also aids in the secretion of the growth hormone.
Growth Hormone Releasing Hormone	Releases the growth hormone.
Growth Hormone	Helps stimulate reproduction of cells and growth.
Leptin	Slows the appetite while simultaneously accelerating metabolic rate
Orexin	Increases appetite, alertness and energy levels Secretin inhibits gastric acid production.

There are dozens of hormones. In fact, they're being discovered on an ongoing basis. We don't really know how many there are.

Hormones are produced by the endocrine glands; the most important of which are the pituitary, thyroid, thymus, adrenals, pancreas, ovaries and testes.

Of these, the pituitary, which is situated at the exact centre of the brain, is considered the Master gland, because it controls the release of many of the body's hormones. For example, it's known that the anterior lobe of the pituitary, which has three lobes, secretes ten hormones that are required for the regulation of growth, for reproduction and to control metabolism.

The hypothalamus, which is considered to be the command centre of the brain, is connected by capillaries to the pituitary. Whereas the pituitary can be seen as a mere instrument panel, that's indifferent to its capacity to release hormones, the hypothalamus appears to communicate with the rest of the body, via signals sent through the nervous system; and it pushes the buttons on the pituitary's control panel by secreting hormone releasing agents. The pituitary then releases hormones which in turn cause the thyroid, adrenals and other glands to release their hormones.

There are Hormones... And Then There are Hormones...

Most of the body's hormones go about their business of keeping us functioning with no decision-making required of our subconscious mind; with no input from our ego mind. The process is 'automatic'. However, some of our hormones are kept to one side in our survival arsenal; for example adrenalin, cortisol and norepinephrine. We need these if we're threatened, or if we perceive that we are threatened.

What makes these stress or 'survival' hormones different is that they can be triggered by the *perception* of a survival threat; and the perceiving is done by our subconscious mind (our ego) in about 1/10,000th of a second. The ego can then trigger the release of these stress hormones into our system.

Stress Hormones are Stressful...

The very purpose of stress hormones is to put the body into a state that is not its preferred state; and that can be harmful to us. Cortisol, for example, is a steroidal hormone. It's considered 'the' stress hormone. It's produced by the adrenal glands.

Cortisol is secreted when the amygdalae perceive a threat and send a warning to the hypothalamus, which in turn releases a 'releasing' hormone (CRH) that tells the pituitary gland to release a hormone (ACTH) to tell the adrenal gland to release cortisol.

The secretion of cortisol into your body is fine when there's an acute (that is, short-term) real-life emergency; but if you're deceived by your misguided ego into perceiving 'survival' threats all the time, in all manner of guises – that is, when you become chronically worried (that is, worried over a prolonged period of time) – your body will continuously release cortisol into your system, and if that happens it's a case of your hormone system sabotaging your own health.

How does this sabotage happen? The fact is you have a number of nervous systems in your body and the two I'm most interested in are:

- The parasympathetic nervous system (PNS)
- The sympathetic nervous system (SNS)

When you're feeling 'unstressed' your PNS is operating and your health will be optimal. For example, your immune system will be operating normally. However, if you're subconsciously, by your ego mind, perceiving ongoing threats then your SNS takes over from the PNS and it shuts down your immune system to make more energy available to fight or flee from the perceived threat.

Of course, if you're immune system goes off line for more than a very short time you're at the very real risk of illness, disease, infection, and so on. In other words, chronic (that is, long-term) stress, even if it exists for an imaginary rather than a real threat to your life, can turn out to be a very real threat to your health and well-being by shutting down your immune system.

The 'Feelings' Agenda...

What I refer to as your emotional brain (the limbic system) is a part of the subconscious brain. However, it's not focused on, or solely on, survival (like the original survival brain). Instead this part of the brain has a big say in:

- Your higher emotions
- Your mood
- Your instinctive feelings
- Your anxieties
- Your pleasure
- Your anger
- Your sexual behaviour
- The attention you subconsciously or automatically give to particular stimuli
- Emotionally-charged memories

These are huge drivers in how you interact with the world, and how you achieve, or fail to achieve, the outcomes your conscious brain is telling you it wants to achieve.

It's 'Yes' or 'No'... No 'Maybe'... No 'Perhaps'...

This emotional brain can be described as a 'yes' and 'no' brain. We know this because as far back as the 1960s the American physician and neuroscientist, Paul MacLean, formulated the three-part brain concept which he discussed at length in his book *The Triune Brain in Evolution*. Neuroscience has adopted MacLean's concept. We looked at this in Chapter 2.

MacLean discovered that as far as this emotional brain is concerned something is either 'agreeable' or 'disagreeable' (that is, something either feels good or it doesn't feel good). The emotional brain 'agrees' with the survival brain that our 'survival' depends on the avoidance of pain and loss (because pain and loss don't feel agreeable or good) and endorses the repetition of what the survival mind (ego) sees as 'agreeable' or 'good'.

Insight: What this means is that apart from being an enormously powerful processer of stimuli your ProtoBrain and your ProtoEgo have leverage over your life's results through the power of feelings or emotions.

Thoughtless Feeler...

The emotional brain is a thoughtless feeler. We know this because neuroscientists have discovered that if your emotional brain is stimulated with mild electrical current, it can spontaneously trigger emotions such as fear, joy, rage, pleasure and pain – it's automatic; a reflex action that occurs without stimuli from the environment.

This tells us that there's a doorway through which your conscious mind can potentially enter and coax your subconscious ego to start reacting in a more desirable manner, from the perspective of what your conscious brain wants you to achieve in your life.

Insight: My belief is that your heart, on the other hand, is a thoughtful feeler; and the most powerful tool you have for positive growth.

Not Analytical...

There's no analysis, no thought involved in the ego's decision-making process; so don't think you can overcome your negative life results merely by calling on your ego mind to start being logical, or reasonable, or realistic, so that you can achieve better results in your life.

Insight: However, if you can coax your ego mind into eliciting the *feelings* that will get it to change for the better the reactive decisions it mechanically makes you are on the right track; because feelings are powerful drivers of how your ego reacts, how it can be steered to get you your consciously desired life outcomes. One way to do this is through your heart.

Someone's Unpredictable... Is it You...?

Your ego is the source of the unpredictable behaviour we all engage in from time to time. If you've ever wondered why you did something that in hindsight seemed foolish, it's your ego that has made the decision – and its decisions are rarely helpful or wise; they just seem to be. After you've acted on that foolish subconscious ego decision your slower conscious brain catches up with what has happened and wonders: why on earth did I do that?

Insight: This tells us that your ego mind is *always* in the driver's seat, with your conscious mind running behind, trying to catch up.

Insight: Although your emotional ego mind has extensive interconnections with your frontal lobe (your conscious brain), it's emotions or feelings, not logic, that steer the decisions you make, that give you the outcomes you're getting in your daily life.

The pivotal role of your emotional ego mind can't be ignored because it appears to eavesdrop on your frontal lobe. It 'feels' whether or not your thinking brain has a 'good' idea or is about to make a good decision or not, and forms an emotional assessment on whether this 'feels right', from the standpoint of your ego mind's existing blueprint for life. If your conscious idea doesn't feel right then your ego mind will subconsciously, instantly, veto it, behind the scenes.

Insight: There's no doubt that, in a given situation, your emotional ego mind *instantly* reports its feelings to the survival ego mind for an *instant* decision to be made on how the ego should 'react' to what your conscious brain is trying to cobble together.

The ProtoBrain Is Wired to be Biased...

Paul MacLean claimed to have found in the emotional brain a *physical* (that is, a *biological*) basis for the dogmatic, paranoid tendencies that sometimes beset every one of us. The emotional mind seems to be a source of irrational subconscious value judgments (prejudices and biases). This finding is further neuroscientific evidence that your ego mind is hard-wired, through its embedded signature filtering and behavioural programmes, to stay in charge and unless you change its embedded programmes, you'll keep getting the same results in life.

The Subconscious Allies Verses the Conscious You...

Accept as a fact, for the purposes of what you want to achieve in life, that the survival ego and the emotional ego (together the ProtoEgo) act as allies, and make decisions for you before your conscious frontal lobe is aware of what's going on. Your thinking brain is far too slow to be a match for your ProtoEgo; and, besides, your thinking brain is only on duty about 3% to 5% of the time.

Insight: However, your heart is potentially more powerful than your mind.

Your Survival Brain Is Busy...

There's no question that your rational, conscious brain is a massive neurological machine. Size-wise, it's bigger than your survival brain, but processing-capacity-wise it's a minnow in comparison.

Insight: Your heart filters and processes information on an entirely different level to your brain.

Insight: It has been estimated that if the human brain were a computer, it could perform 38,000 trillion operations per second whereas the world's most powerful super computers, the IBM Blue Gene series, can manage only .002% of this.

Insight: It seems that your survival brain is about 500,000 times more powerful at processing stimuli than your conscious brain.

The jobs your survival brain Is attending to 24/7...
Check out this list of some of the jobs that your busy survival brain Is handling around the clock to keep you alive...

- It's looking after the needs of the approximately 70 trillion individual cells in your body
- It processes 20 million environmental stimuli per second – while your modern, conscious mind can process only about 40 stimuli per second – which means your subconscious brain is about 500,000 times more powerful than your rational, conscious brain
- It's creating antibodies to fight disease and infection threats

- It's making and releasing hormones to send chemical signals around your body and building proteins that trigger your 70 trillion cells to undertake necessary tasks on the cellular level
- It's constantly eavesdropping on your rational, conscious brain
- It oversees countless complex vital bodily organs that themselves are constantly busy, such as your heart (which beats around 100,000 times per day or almost 40 million heart beats per year) pumping blood through 100,000 kilometres (60,000 miles) of vascular networks that your subconscious brain is also managing
- It's watching every one of your blood cells, each of which makes a complete circuit through your body every 20 to 60 seconds, and it makes sure that the 3 million red blood cells you lose every minute of your life are being replaced
- Each second of every day it supervises about 100,000 chemical reactions that take place in each of the 70 trillion cells in your body
- It ensures that the 10 million of your cells that die every second are mostly replaced and it carries out repairs on tens of millions of others
- It looks after the 100 billion neurons in your brain, including those in your neocortex (your rational conscious brain) as well as the neurons in the rest of your body
- It operates all your bodily systems such as your autonomic nervous system and maintains your homeostasis

Insight: It's not surprising that with this non-stop workload your subconscious brain isn't just sitting around waiting to process bright ideas from your conscious mind. Unless the thought bubbles in your conscious mind are seen by the subconscious as relevant to what it does – which is to make sure you 'survive' – it discards them in a flash.

Your Subconscious Brain Doesn't Know it but it's 'Spirally Dynamic'...

In ancient times (let's call them *ProtoTimes*) survival meant having food, shelter, protection from predators and danger and the opportunity to mate.

'Survival' today is more complex. Our survival checklist has been expanded due to the dramatic changes in our life conditions. These changes have also resulted in wholesale changes in our values. To understand what 'survival' means to your *conscious* and to your *subconscious* (your ego) requires a detour into spiral dynamics.

Spiral Dynamics is a subject beyond the scope of this book, but it's worth a brief overview; so I'll mention a few salient points, to give you an insight into what you need to know to get to understand why your aspirational conscious mind and your subconscious ego don't seem to see eye-to-eye:

- These-days, we westerners live in advanced societies where basic survival needs (food, shelter and protection from most predators – let's forget the banksters and Wall Street for now) are mostly provided by central organisations (such as governments) or specialist suppliers (such as farmers) or service providers in exchange for money (such as the taxes you pay in various forms) and the money you fork out at the supermarket
- Our relationship with the opposite sex is still a paramount concern because we have a subconscious biological drive to procreate
- We consciously or subconsciously 'know' and 'feel' that the level of social status e achieve will affect our level of comfort and safety, where we live, our quality of food, our choice of mate, our lifestyle and our other life opportunities
- Today, social status can be bought, which means fiat money is a top priority for most of us, male and female. So anything that can help us make more money or maintain a level of income (to maintain a particular level of lifestyle) is a guaranteed point of focus for all of us
- Today many of us don't trust fiat currency or the share market so we're looking for alternatives to both protect our wealth (without relying on fiat currency) and guarantee cash flow (with fiat currency or, say, cryptos)
- These-days, females have far more personal aspirations than in previous generations, so having an independent source of income is as important to them – it's a 'survival' issue for them – as it is to their partners
- We now need not only to provide for the basic needs of our off-spring but to educate them at enormous expense to give them a chance to make it in our insecure, competitive and ever more complex society – and that also requires a lot of money
- Today, we live in a world of cyclic economic uncertainty with no job security, so to survive many of us will jump at the chance to become

financially free – or even get off the grid – which means, once again, that we think one of our top values or top priorities is getting our hands on as much money as possible

- Many of us have to travel long distances to work (often hundreds or even thousands of kilometres), spending prolonged periods away from our families or friends – and most of those that do this want to find a way to make the income they need that lets them stay closer to home

- Most of us (about 97%) have unending money challenges such as with our mortgage (or rent), health costs, lack of savings for retirement and the everyday high cost of living – we're always looking for ways to supplement our income so we don't retire 'broke' (that is, so we don't have to curb our lifestyle in retirement)

- Huge numbers of us suffer from 'chronic' (meaning 'long-term') stress of greater or lesser severity, and this interferes with our ability to achieve our life's goals, as well as adversely affecting our health

- We contend with countless social problems such as crime, substance abuse, mental illness and lifestyle illnesses such as diabetes for ourselves or our loved ones

We have to deal with these modern survival issues with a survival mind (ego) that's not cut out for it. Hundreds of millions of us are constantly looking for solutions to these problems – what I call *ProtoStressers* – but we're doing it with a decision-making subconscious mind (ego) that's not actually programmed for the task.

ProtoStressers And Your Subconscious Ego Mind...

You can be fairly sure that the following list of items are either consciously attracting your attention – when your conscious mind is actually on duty – and are always on the radar for your subconscious paranoid ego:

- For all of us, the avoidance of 'pain' is by far the most important driver that gets us to do or not do something. It just depends on the threshold of the pain required for each of us to trigger action

- For all of us, protection from loss or 'predators' (in all guises) for ourselves, our partners and our off-spring is an ever-present concern – at least subconsciously for our ego – but, again, our subconscious

doesn't have the programmes to deal with the modern versions of these threats
- Whether you admit it or not, we're all subconsciously concerned about sexual procreation, and not just for the continuation of our personal gene pool, and this can be a cause of anxiety and chronic stress
- We all want to *feel* that we have power over our lives, but very few of us do

Insight: However, there are some who have far more control over what happens to them, at least on a worldly level, than the overwhelming majority of people – and it doesn't boil down to a question of money. It boils down to how they re-programme their subconscious ego mind.

Why Your ProtoBrain Rules… And Your Conscious Mind Doesn't…

In the table, below, you'll see how your ProtoBrain differs from your modern, conscious rational brain. This is stuff you need to know if you want to start a meaningful dialogue with your subconscious ego mind in order to improve your lot in life.

Subconscious ProtoBrain (non-rational)	Modern Conscious Brain (rational thinking)
Active 100% of the time Never off-duty Never asleep	Usually active only 3%-5% of the time May get up to 10% in short bursts for some people
Super high-speed processor – can process about 20 million stimuli per second	Slow processor – can process only about 40 stimuli per second
Can multi-task	Can't multi-task
Hard-wired/automatic	Neuroplastic (that is, flexible) but 'controlled'
Limited attention span unless under threat	When active, has a good attention span, is imaginative and creative
Reactive	Responsive
Reflexive	Reflective
Has hard-wired signature filtering and behavioural programmes/loops – blueprints that it slavishly follows Not capable of consistent decisions, by choice. Its world view is limited by the information that is available at a given moment (that it doesn't filter out) and therefore it cannot be consistent Often makes bad decisions	Is not limited by the information available at a given moment – can refer to its database of knowledge/experience. Can make consistent decisions Has the ability to create unlimited new thought and feedback loops for the ProtoBrain – if it doesn't do so then, by default, the ProtoBrain's 'mechanical' decision making is in control

Dismisses (that is, filters out) a lot of valuable information	
Has limited feedback mechanisms for available information/stimuli	Can create unlimited new feedback mechanisms
Can't comprehend beyond what it 'feels' is necessary for ProtoSurvival	Can comprehend well beyond base survival needs
Initiates production of hormones (drugs) in our body to reward us for complying with its habitual programmes even when they're not good for us It will release stress hormones if we make a rational, conscious decision that's inconsistent with its hardwired programmes even if those decisions are good for us	Has the capacity to re-wire the ProtoBrain, to alter its habits or default filtering systems and behavioural patterns
Is the home of our comfort and discomfort zones It's the home of our upper limits – they hold us back from reaching our potential and can destroy our lives	Can get our ProtoBrain to break through its discomfort zone ceiling and change our ProtoBrain upper limits Can enable us to reach our potential and enhance our lives
Impulsive Feelings driven Biased and paranoid	Logical Thought driven Neutral and analytical
Senses stimuli	Perceives and conceives both environmental and non-environmental stimuli
Will fight harder to prevent loss than to achieve gains	Will strategize, weigh options Can be extremely determined or totally wavering
Effort-less Automatic	Effort-full Directed
Associative	Rule-governed
Rigid Habitual Slow learning	Flexible Open-minded Quick learning
Never consciously aware Intuitive decision-maker Makes 'snap' decisions	Consciously aware when switched 'on' Deliberative in its conclusions Weighs alternatives Analytical – the little voice we hear in our head that talks when, for example, we're adding numbers

What You Learned in This Chapter

- Your conscious mind and your subconscious ego mind aren't reading from the same user manual
- Your subconscious ego will *always* have its all-powerful survival agenda
- Your ProtoBrain and your ProtoEgo aren't interested in your conscious dreams, your conscious values or your conscious passions
- Your subconscious ego mind has an awesome arsenal of weapons, hormonal and emotional, that it can and will use to get its own way, whether or not that's good for you
- As a raw processor of vast amounts of stimuli your ProtoBrain has no peer and it's at the disposal of your ego – and your conscious mind is no match for it
- Your conscious mind is under constant surveillance by your mysterious inner 'big brother' (ego); but it is possible to outfox the ego because it can't think, evaluate or strategize like your logical brain
- Your subconscious ego mind can't tell the difference between truth and fiction, wants to believe stuff, is curious and has the fantastic ability to emote – and you can use all of these traits to your advantage – its embedded signature filtering and behavioural programmes constitute an impressive firewall but it's not impregnable
- You need to know more about Spiral Dynamics
- You need to know more about your enigmatic heart

Chapter 4

Ancestral Memories... Archaic ProtoEgo Behaviour... Awareness and Self-Awareness...

What You'll Discover in This Chapter...

- Your ProtoEgo (the subconscious survival and subconscious emotional mind) is aware but not *self*-aware, which means it's not suited to making decisions, by itself, about your wellbeing in the 21st century
- Only the frontal lobe part of your neocortex is self-aware and capable of delivering a better life to you
- Your subconscious ProtoEgo has a form of intelligence but its intelligence is not capable of enabling you to grow, in consciousness, and thereby achieve better outcomes in life
- The capacity for intelligence you have in your frontal lobe is of a different nature to your subconscious intelligence and unless you engage your conscious intelligence in your decision-making you cannot achieve your conscious goals
- How you use your time defines who you are

You've Got Two Personalities... At Least Two...

Our subconscious ProtoEgo is self-absorbed, inward-looking, suspicious and paranoid. On the other hand, our conscious frontal lobe is open-minded, compassionate and thoughtful – largely because it can communicate with your heart.

These are like two adversaries vying for control of you, and the question for you is: when it comes to your future 'happiness' which one is best able to guide you and which will win?

Insight: I've used the word 'happiness' because I can't think of a better way to get this point across; but I'm not 'happy' that it's the correct word, because it has connotations of ego. To me true happiness can only derive from the heart; not the ego. Whilst you have ego your happiness is of a lower kind; usually material or based on ego love. But that's another story, not for this book.

Your subconscious ProtoBrain is powerful, fast, efficient and that enables your ProtoEgo to be a potential threat to you because it has control of your inner hormonal arsenal; which means it controls the levers of your parasympathetic nervous system ('PNS') and your sympathetic nervous system ('SNS').

To compound the problem, your subconscious ProtoBrain and your ProtoEgo are on duty 24/7 whereas your frontal lobe is only switched on about 3% to 5% of the time.

Insight: Although your heart is on-line 24/7 that's no good to you unless you're engaging it.

How You Create You... Your Critical Faculty...

Everything you encounter, every situation you experience, is compared by your subconscious mind (ego) with your existing subconscious knowledge base and if it doesn't find a match with what you already 'know' your ProtoEgo is likely to reject new information as unfamiliar, unsafe, wrong or untrustworthy and therefore dangerous or irrelevant to you.

When I talk about your existing subconscious knowledge base, I'm including in this:

- Your subconscious awareness of things you cannot currently do.
- Your self-imposed subconscious upper limits on what you're prepared to do.
- Your embedded subconscious biases and fears.

These subconscious comparisons your ProtoEgo constantly undertakes are part of your inbuilt survival mechanism. It has the result that your ProtoEgo will only want to rely on and act on that which it sees as familiar, proven and trustworthy, unless you can 'safely' trigger its natural curiosity to venture a little further, or into a new space – but the problem is that the yardstick by which it makes these decisions is often flawed because its fundamental beliefs and biases are flawed. The result is that the system you rely on, that's meant to protect and nurture you, is your inner stumbling block.

The end result of this flawed process is that your conscious mind will ratify the bad decisions made by your subconscious mind. You won't act on an idea rejected by your ProtoEgo, even if it should not have been rejected; even if your frontal lobe had a better idea; one that could transform your life for the better.

So, for example, if you believe you cannot do something (such as lead a healthier lifestyle), then any suggestion that you can will tend to be disbelieved and distrusted by your ProtoEgo, and hence by you. Your subconscious mind will veto the idea and your conscious mind will ratify the bad decision by telling you, "No, that's not for me... it doesn't' feel right."

Alternatively, you may go through the motions of trying the new idea, but do so with the expectation of failure; and failure is what you'll get if you do something half-heartedly, with the inner expectation of failure. Your ProtoEgo will subconsciously set out to fail just to prove it's right and your frontal lobe is wrong.

Sadly, having 'proved' that you are indeed unable to apply this new knowledge you thereby reinforce your self-imposed limitations and deny yourself the opportunity to grow. Your ProtoEgo will have just put stronger locks on the prison it has built for you.

Henry Ford (1863-1947), the founder of the Ford Motor Company, captured this reality of human nature when he famously said, "Whether you think you can or think you can't you're probably right."

Conscious Critical Faculty...

This self-limiting mechanism is often referred to as the 'conscious critical faculty'. The good news is that the conscious critical faculty can be by-passed. Hypnotherapists (not to be confused with hypnotists) are psychotherapists (usually psychologists) who utilise hypnotherapy to make people more amenable to new ideas, and new ways of thinking, to overcome many issues including anxiety, bad habits, lack of confidence, low self-esteem, and so on.

Your critical faculty isn't a physical barrier in your head. It's not even an organ. Nor is it a disease or illness. It's just an embedded subconscious ProtoEgo programme that's meant to 'protect' you by ensuring you don't do anything you're not already programmed to do in a particular situation.

Babies are Born Free...

The critical faculty barrier is almost non-existent when you're born; which is why babies can learn to swim and can learn several languages at the same time. Hence the saying that if you have a child until he's five years old you have him forever; because everything an infant experiences goes straight into his or her subconscious where it forms 'impressions' or concepts from which his or her signature behavioural loops will develop and from which his or her comfort zones will develop.

Your Multiple Comfort Zones...

You have more than one subconscious comfort zone. You have one for every key aspect of your life: relationships, work, learning, dealing with 'chaos' (that is, sudden, unexpected changes in your life's circumstances) and so on. Your comfort zone for one area (such as dealing with people) may be flexible and for another (such as getting rid of bad habits) may be narrow and rigid.

Resistance Is Normal When You Want to Change...

Because of your critical faculty programming during your formative years – which never really end – you can expect to feel subconscious resistance from within even when you consciously desire change. That's normal for all of us, including me, so don't let that worry you. Just accept it as part of the journey of change.

Insight: Once you start on your journey of change don't be disheartened when you still get outcomes or results you don't want. That's your ProtoEgo fighting back. It will take time. Remember you have the time to change just as much as you have the time to remain the same.

You are What You've Been Programmed to be...

As a result of our embedded subconscious programmes we interact with the world (our relationships, work, spending habits and how we spend or mis-spend our time) through our subconscious filters that either exclude new information or new ideas or allow new information or ideas to be acted on.

People who consistently fail are programmed (self-programmed) to fail; and they can be re-programmed (self-programmed) to succeed.

Getting Permission to By-Pass the Critical Faculty Barrier...

It's possible to by-pass your critical faculty, but you need the permission of your ProtoEgo to do this. There are several ways this permission can be obtained. It's done every day by millions of people.

First, it's done in consumer selling. Marketers, for example, have studied the subconscious and know that one way to get past the critical faculty barrier is by making your subconscious curious – by enthralling it with images and stories (like the images and stories in television advertisements) that evoke emotion (that is, feelings), such as the feeling that you must have product X in your life if you are to have the right self-image (that is, if you are to 'survive').

The second way to by-pass the critical faculty barrier is by agreement, such as agreeing to hypnotherapy.

A third way, according to some people, is the use of subliminal messages. As the first part of the word suggests (that is, the prefix 'sub') subliminal messages are believed by their proponents to pass below (sub) the normal limits of perception of the conscious mind but remain discernible by the subconscious.

Insight: Inaudible noises and images not perceived consciously can affect us subconsciously without them being subliminal. If we can see or hear it, even if we don't consciously notice it, it's not subliminal; rather it's supraliminal. One the other hand, we can't consciously perceive subliminal messages even if we're on the alert for them.

Insight: I won't go into subliminal messaging for the purposes of this book because I don't believe it has anything of value to offer you in understanding or overcoming your ProtoEgo.

However, the best way to by-pass your ego is with your most powerful tool: your heart.

Your Inner Crocodile...

What you need to understand is that your ProtoEgo has archaic behavioural programmes that are no more advanced than those of a crocodile. It's ritualistic, rigid and obsessive; and that's likely the source of your problems in life.

What Mistake...?

The ProtoEgo doesn't learn from past mistakes. It will make the same mistakes endlessly, oblivious to your conscious yearnings to do things in a more constructive way.

Warning! Warning...! Your Value Judgments Aren't Rational...!

The emotional mind actually subordinates what you think, consciously, below what you feel subconsciously, making you erratic in what you value; and therefore, how you behave and what you aspire to.

Dangerous Biological Default Settings...

According to Paul MacLean (who devised the triune brain concept) this is a worrying situation because it means that our lowly feelings-charged emotional mind is biologically wired to be in control.

Your Instincts Rule...

Underneath the timebomb of your emotional mind (that is, your limbic or mammalian brain) is your genetically encoded instinctual brain, your survival brain; and its buddy, your ProtoEgo. They're primitive. The ProtoEgo's agenda is to explore its environment, feed, fight or flee if threatened, to dominate its 'rivals' and to procreate.

Self-Awareness...

Self-awareness, at least at the worldly level, is the thinking skill (that is, it's conscious brain stuff) that focuses on your ability to judge your own behaviour and performance and respond appropriately to social situations; which is something your archaic crocodile ProtoEgo will never learn to do. To succeed you have to be self-aware as much as you possibly can. If you're still failing then it just means that you're not yet sufficiently self-aware.

Testing... Testing...

People are often tested on how self-aware they are because it's realised that with self-awareness comes the power to change who we are, to achieve more constructive things out of life – in other words to have a far more fulfilling life.

To be self-aware you have to be more in your conscious realm, operating less on your subconscious defaults. In the self-awareness state you are aware that you're consciously thinking about yourself, about who and what you are.

Insight: You can never make your survival brain, emotional brain or ProtoEgo *self*-aware. They're *aware* of stimuli and sensations but they have no concept of being *self*-aware.

Insight: You don't need to make your ProtoEgo *self*-aware in order to change your behaviour and outcomes, to get a more fulfilled life. You need only re-programme it like you would re-programme a computer. Unfortunately, the apparent ability of a computer not to co-operate with you when you've got an urgent task to complete is nothing compared to your ProtoEgo's ability to hang on to its archaic behavioural programmes. In other words, you *can* change, but don't expect it to be easy.

True Self-Awareness and Socially Engineered Self-Awareness... They're not the Same...

Like me, you've been socially engineered to the point where you've got very little idea who you really are. For now, I want you to remember the figures 97% and 3%. You're probably currently in the 97% of the population that isn't financially independent or 'free', and your ProtoEgo is responsible for that.

Ask yourself this: can I quit work, right now, and live the rest of my life comfortably, maintaining my desired lifestyle without having to sell-off assets or borrow? If your answer is in the negative then you're not financially independent. If one of your aims is to change your outcomes in life (which will necessitate changing how you behave) so that you can move from the 97% and join the 3% who are financially free you have to confront your ProtoEgo.

Road-Testing Your Self-Awareness...

Now that we've had this very brief overview of who you are, with your biological default settings in operation, take the little test, below. It will give you a chance to evaluate yourself and to see yourself as others might see you.

You could ask a couple of candid, objective friends or family to score this test for you, but for the time being it's enough if you do it yourself – and I'll explain the reasons why a little later.

With this test you'll use a scale of 1 to 10, with 10 being 'very', 5 being 'moderately' and 1 being 'barely'.

No	Question on your self-awareness	Self-rating 1-10
1	Rate your ability to overcome life's hardships, like being rejected or told you're wrong	
2	Rate your ability to cope satisfactorily if you lost your job	
3	Rate how happy your relationships with your partner, children and work colleagues are	
4	Rate how sensitive you are to criticism. Does it fire up your emotional ProtoEgo or just get calmly dealt with by your conscious brain?	
5	Rate the extent to which you're in a peer group that is made up of self-aware high-achieving people	
6	Rate the extent to which self-aware people look to you for your opinion, advice or suggestions	
7	Rate your ability to depend on you to deliver on what you promise to you. Are you a quitter, or an excuse-maker?	
8	Rate the extent to which you avoid people who are negative. Do you stick with them even when they hold you back?	
9	To what extent are you generally optimistic about life?	
10	To what extent are you envious of what others have?	
11	To what extent do you think you're a socially engineered puppet?	
12	To what extent do you try to improve the lives of others by selfless giving?	
13	Do you read books? If so, to what extent do you read self-improvement books rather than fiction?	
14	To what extent do you spend your free time just watching TV or playing games when you have free time?	
15	To what extent are you a social media junkie? Do you use social media just for work communications? To what extent is it a means for you to tell the world all about yourself, your children and hobbies?	
16	To what extent do you read contrarian books on investing, economics and so on?	

Self-Awareness Tests You've Already Done… Or not Done…

Be careful with self-awareness tests. Most are designed by people who are within the 97% for other people who are also within the 97%, but more on that later, when we look, briefly, at the 'blue level' in Spiral Dynamics.

51

Insight: Being conformed to the 97% is a problem if you're looking for self-awareness and better outcomes in life. Unfortunately, your ProtoEgo is a victim of social engineering which means your ProtoEgo wants to keep you within the 97%.

What You Learned in This Chapter...

- Awareness and self-awareness aren't the same.
- Only self-awareness gives you choices in life.
- Time is your greatest gift.
- You can overcome your critical faculty barriers.

Chapter 5
'Power' Beats 'Force'...

What You'll Discover in This Chapter...

- You live in a universe of energy and it can be both positive (that is, based on power) and negative (that is, reliant on force)
- To get the best outcomes in life you have to know how you cause positive and negative energy in your life
- Negative energy (force) can only operate negatively, can give you only negative outcomes in life
- Positive energy (power) can only operate positively, can give you only positive outcomes in life
- The entire structure of positive and negative energy you have and you project is governed by your own levels of consciousness
- At the centre of this choice between power (which is your friend) and force (which is not your friend) is your ego

Kinesiology...

'Kinesiology' comes from the Greek *kinesis* meaning 'movement' and *kinein* meaning 'to move' and *logia* meaning 'study'. Today, kinesiology involves combining principles of anatomy, neuroscience and biomechanics, and it's now a mainstay of orthopaedics.

The practice of kinesiology is aimed at teaching the body to adapt or modify how it functions so that you get improved performance, and that necessitates rewiring the ProtoBrain using programmes of physical activity (that is, exercises). This can involve aerobic exercise, anaerobic strength training, flexibility training, balance and so on.

It's apparently been clinically shown that these programmes can reduce depression, reduce the risk of cardiovascular disease and improve sleep and generally improve your entire physical well-being; and it all comes from within your ProtoBrain, which is overseen by your ProtoEgo.

Dr David Hawkins... A New Direction... Behavioural Kinesiology...?

According to David Hawkins (psychiatrist and physician), in the late 1970s, studies in behavioural (as opposed to physical or motor) aspects of kinesiology showed that indicator muscles (that is, certain muscles that were subjected to testing so as to give data or measurements) would strengthen or weaken in response to the subject's positive or negative reaction or response to emotional and intellectual, as well as physical, stimuli.

For example, a smile would make the test result stronger and a negative thought or statement, such as, "I hate you!" would make it weaker.

How the Kinesiological Testing Works...

It involves two people: the subject and the investigator or verifier; and the sequence is well understood and has been practised for decades. I go into the process in detail in Chapter 17 of this book.

I've known of it since the 1980s. I can remember a herbalist I used to go to for herbal health supplement mixtures, made from herbs grown in his own huge herb farm, using this technique with me many times as he moved quickly with me along benches of literally hundreds of litre-sized bottles of liquefied herbs. I could actually feel the power in my shoulder strengthen or weaken as his hand passed over various herb mixtures.

So, as far as one's physiological needs are concerned, I believe it works.

But What About Kinesiology and Consciousness...?

Leaving aside the physical aspects of the practice of kinesiology, which in my own experience seem to work, things took a sudden, dramatic turn in 1975 when Hawkins began research into the kinesiological aspects of truth and untruth.

The details and results of his findings are covered in his many books (such as *Power v's Force, Healing and Recovery, Truth v's Falsehood, Reality, Spirituality and Modern Man*, and so on).

Hawkins concluded that there appeared to be a communal 'consciousness', a spiritus mundi, which, using the language of Carl Jung (1875-1961), Hawkins called a 'database of consciousness' referring to a perceived shared sub-rational knowledge and wisdom.

Kinesiology and Truth and Falsehood...

Hawkins said that he found that questions used with his test subjects must be phrased so that the answer is clearly 'yes' or 'no', like a nerve synapse that is either 'on' or 'off', 'open' or 'closed'. If correct, this finding tells us that our basic cellular (that is anatomical) knowledge, wisdom and know-how are 'yes' or 'no', not 'maybe'. There's only black and white, no grey.

Insight: Don't equate the 'yes' and 'no', 'true' and 'false' model with the 'right' and 'wrong', 'good' and 'bad' judgments or pronouncements of man that are so typically found in the Blue system of the Spiral Dynamics spiral. They're not the same.

According to Hawkins, the kinesiological concept as applied to 'consciousness' is clinically, extensively, tried and proven and is squarely based on a fundamental universal energy, power, wisdom and truth; whereas man's judgments of 'right' and 'wrong', spring from an absence of truth, lack of wisdom, and from man's application of force rather than him tapping into the universe's power.

Insight: Hawkins' test is not fool proof. There are limits to how it can be used; as I show, in particular, in Chapter 16.

Kinesiological Calibrations of Truth and Power...

Hawkins said that his clinical research led to him being able to actually test and calibrate a scale of relative truth by which virtually everything man gets up to or theorises about – such as Keynesian economics, the theory of evolution, political or spiritual ideologies and philosophies, social conditioning constructs, and so on – can be tested for their universal veracity or falsehood. On Hawkins' Map of Consciousness (MoC) his calibration scale ranges from 1 to 1000 and works logarithmically. Although his scale stops at 1000, he says it actually has no upper limit that he ascertained.

The MoC... A Calibration of Physical Self-Awareness...

The reason I'm interested in the results of Hawkins' work is that, within some limits, it seems to reveal truths about our levels of physical awareness which will be inextricably interwoven with whether we operate from a solid foundation of power (anabolically) or a quagmire of force (catabolically).

Insight: Anabolic means 'life-enhancing' whereas catabolic means 'life-consuming', and this is an apt metaphor for how you can live your life. You can live in a life-enhancing way or in a life-consuming way. In fact, you're doing one or the other right now; and you will be tomorrow, next month, next year and so on.

Others Have Tried Kinesiology...

The concepts, the truths, that have been revealed by Hawkins' work have apparently been examined by scientists working in the fields of theoretical physics, nonlinear dynamics and chaos theory; but I cannot say what their conclusions were.

Insight: It has long since been postulated that Hawkins' findings have potential application in politics, commerce, medicine, sociology, the natural sciences, history and even art. Its empirical applications in psychology, philosophy and religious lines of enquiry are also being promoted. Whether any of these is correct remains to be seen, in my view.

With qualifications, that I'll go into later, Hawkins' findings are a potential source of valuable information for you when it comes to your ego and your level of consciousness.

Cynicism and Scepticism V Belief...

People can, for the purposes of Hawkins' work, and this book, be generally classified as believers and non-believers; optimists and pessimists; the open-minded and the sceptics.

It could be said that to the sceptics, regardless of the source of the evidence, their glass is not half full but half empty; everything is dubious, they won't believe it until they see it. These people are frightened, small (in heart) and doomed. Theirs is a catabolic life.

It could also be said that to the open-minded, their glass is not half empty but half-*full*; everything presented in good faith is accepted as likely to be true unless proven false. These people are courageous, big (in heart) and destined to keep growing, in spite of set-backs. Theirs is an anabolic life.

Insight: The answer is to research the subject with an open mind rather than apply your biases.

Newtonian Reality V Quantum (Holistic) Reality...

This isn't a book about physics, so I'll keep this short and then get back to you and me and our ProtoEgo stuff.

When Einstein famously said, "$E = mc^2$" he was recognising that energy and matter are one and the same. The formula means: energy (E) equals matter (m, mass) multiplied by the speed of light squared (c^2). Einstein had realised that we don't live in a universe of discrete physical objects separated by dead space; as is envisaged by linear Newtonian physics. He realised that the universe is one indivisible, dynamic whole, in which energy and matter are so deeply entwined that it's impossible to consider them as independent elements; which is what Newtonian physics does.

Insight: It's getting to the stage that today's physicists are suggesting that matter is an illusion, because they say we now know that atoms have no physical structure! Atoms are actually made up of invisible energy, not of tangible matter!

Map of Consciousness (MoC)... An Anatomy of Consciousness...

This brings us back to David Hawkins and his Map of Consciousness (MoC). By now you should realise that Hawkins would say that his MoC puts us at the door to consciousness, to power. We'll look at that proposition more closely; but, for now let's consider where our life's outcomes originate.

To Eliminate Unwanted Effects, You Have to Eliminate Ineffective Decisions…

The reason so many of us fail to find the answers to important questions, such as 'why am I not financially independent?', isn't due to a lack of data, or evidence, but rather to:

- Our propensity to accept the Spiral Dynamics Blue system's arbitrary intellectual foundations, such as the wisdom of Keynesian economics, as reflecting reality, or even common sense
- A failure to pose the correct questions with the result that we cannot find answers

Insight: Spiral Dynamics theory says there are various tiers, each of six levels of values. At present it's safe to say as a generalisation that the western world is operating from the fourth level (the Blue level) of the first tier.

First Tier Colours	Life Conditions	Mind/Coping Strategies/Values
Beige Commenced 40,000+ years ago	Biological, primitive, ProtoEgo, urges and drives – physical sensors dictate the state of being	ProtoEgo survival. Life reliant on natural instincts
Purple Commenced 40,000 years ago	Tribal. Life is threatening and full of mysterious powers and spirit beings that must be placated and appeased	The spirits are placated by sacrifices. Things are 'right' or 'wrong' according to the ritual/ law that maintains the status quo. Magic, law, lore and tradition. Ritualistic and animistic
Red Commenced 10,000 years ago	Power gods. The strong prevail and the week serve. Nature is to be conquered and subdued	Egocentric. The emphasis on dominance, conquest and power. Seize and exploit
Blue Commenced 6,000–4,000 years ago	This is the current, mainstream western system of government. 'Blue' doesn't like to 'exploit' people but it wants to 'control' them. There is a culture of absolute 'right' and 'wrong'. The masses are controlled by a higher authority that punishes crime and promises eventual rewards for complying with the system (e.g., pensions in retirement, free medical, etc) but the	Absolutism. Obedience to government. Rules driven. One conforms or is an outsider. Social conditioning is at its peak

	promises may not be fulfilled. Belief in righteous living	
Orange Commenced 700 years ago	People in orange are entrepreneurial. They've learnt that people in the blue system can be a source of high income for goods and services. Emphasis on materialism and prosperity. People with the orange mindset want financial freedom and as much independence as possible	The age of science and exploitation. Age of high intellectual achievement and growing atheism and humanism
Green Commenced 150 years ago	Nature has changed from being threatening to being a habitat where humanity can find purpose and love through sharing and co-operation. Holistic medicine is common. People in the green system will likely be environmentalists and believers in eastern spiritual practices. They syncretise spiritual beliefs	There is concern about exploitation of the environment. There is a sense of the need for stewardship of the environment. The system tends to be leaderless, rudderless, consensual and completely unworkable

Second Tier Colours	Life Conditions	Mind/Coping Strategies/Values
Yellow Commenced 50 years ago	'Chaotic' – meaning that there is constant change in how we live and people need to be able to cope with the change or they can be left behind. Uncertainty is an accepted state of the life conditions	This tends to be the place where you would find free, integrated thinkers who are existential in beliefs, questioning, accepting. This is the level that astute entrepreneurs from the orange level would seek to live in once they've made their millions. Principled, economic and belief in personal freedom
Turquoise Not yet commenced	Delicately balanced, interlocking forces where the Earth is in man's hands	Seeks order from the 'chaos' (constantly changing conditions). Holistic, experiential, collaborative. A person in the turquoise system would not be part of the world as we know it. They would possibly live separately from the rank and file who had not yet achieved the turquoise mindset
Coral Not yet commenced	We cannot yet predict what the life conditions would be at this level	We cannot predict the neurological capacities or the beliefs that people will have. This is a level for the future

Notes:

1. Each level of the spiral is judgmental in its own right. People's egos vary according to the level they are at.

2. In today's west, most people (probably 97%) live within the blue system, although they may exhibit entrepreneurialism (orange) by having their own business. They may exhibit 'green' by supporting environmentalism.

3. People can be at different levels according to which aspect of their life they're dealing with. They might be in the middle of blue when it comes to 'law and order' but be 'greenies' when it comes to the environment. As far as their personal relationships are concerned, they could wax and wane. This is why the model works as a spiral that is dynamic rather than as a layer cake.

4. People who exhibit orange and green tendencies differ from the people who live only at the blue level in that they can think outside the blue system.

5. Each of the levels operates as either a 'I, me, my' level or an 'us, we, our' level. They alternate, so that, for example, beige, red, orange and yellow are 'I, me, my' levels whereas purple, blue and green are 'us, we, our' levels.

6. The only way you can understand precisely where you fit would be to undergo the two key Spiral Dynamics tests: the values profile test and the change state indicator test.

Where do Solutions Come From...?

You cannot find solutions to the ineffective results in your life in the Spiral Dynamics Blue system by asking questions devised by Blue system 'wisdom'. You have to step outside (above) the Blue system in order to be able to see clearly. So, conventional Blue system wisdom on most topics is unhelpful.

Blue system babble just creates more Blue system 'wisdom'. The result is that the Blue system like the levels that precede it on the Spiral (Beige, Purple and Red) falls back on using *force* and is unable to tap into *power* and as force is negative it can only ever give negative effects.

The Spiral Dynamics Blue system (like the Beige, Purple and Red systems) is ineffective because it's founded on force; and you are ineffective because the Blue system is the home of your ProtoEgo. You have been socially conditioned by and into the Blue system.

Insight: Your ego and your intellect are products of the Spiral Dynamics Blue system or level.

The Difference Between Power and Force...

According to David Hawkins, force is a lower mind phenomenon, found in the Blue system is experienced through the senses and is expressed by reactive decisions whereas the power of higher mind consciousness can be tapped into only through awareness. So what are the signposts of awareness?

The answer according to Hawkins is that the non-linear (non-Newtonian) fields of enquiry have more potential for breakthroughs to 'consciousness' or 'enlightenment' (but not to the purpose of human life) than conventional linear (Newtonian) science.

Since Newton's time things have changed a lot; for example we now have:

• kinesiology – which, for the first time, has exposed the intimate connection between mind and body

- advanced computing – which has enabled the depiction and analysis of vast amounts of data, which has disclosed systems previously considered to be indecipherable 'chaos' by linear Newtonian physics
- analysis of chaos data – which has identified energy patterns that have been named 'attractors' – the existence of which had been postulated by advanced non-linear equations mathematics
- fractal geometry – whereas the classical school geometry was all about 'smooth' shapes (such as circles and triangles) fractal geometry is about more complex, 'rough', shapes, not even considered by the fathers of classical geometry: Pythagoras, Plato and Euclid
- psychiatry – which is the most non-linear field of medicine, examining such concepts as intuition, decision-making and human behaviour – all of which is ProtoEgo stuff

Insight: In my belief, the reason the non-linear fields of science hold lots of answers about us is that all human life potential, experiences and processes are probably non-linear. On the other hand, base physical survival is probably linear.

Back to Hawkins' Map of Consciousness (MoC)...

According to Hawkins, possibly one of the greatest advances in human psychology has come about because of the discovery that kinesiology potentially opens the door to understanding our levels of consciousness. In this context the MoC is worthy of a closer look, because it might tell us something about the ego.

In the table, below, I give you a summary of how the MoC operates, as I see it, for the purpose of this book.

Remember, according to Hawkins, the key crossover level of consciousness (LoC) is LoC 200, on his MoC. Until you reach LoC 200 you are operating from the weak foundation of force (catabolic). Power (the anabolic foundation) does not begin to emerge until LoC 200; and then gradually increases, logarithmically.

MoC Level	% of mankind at thIs level	Hallmarks of these levels of consciousness	Weaknesses of these levels of consciousness
Below 200 Below 200 Is the level	85% of humankind	No strengths (no power) at these levels. Below 200 is a catabolic (destructive to life) state Home of the ProtoEgo	Based on ProtoEgo force, not power. Causes counterforce, conflict – polarises rather than unifies. Prideful, aggressive, cynical, blames others.

of force and base survival		Lacking integrity, corrupt, selfish, cheating, lying, stealing. There may be 'love' (small 'l'), but Hawkins says there is nothing like the Love (large 'L') of MoC level 500 and beyond.	Judgmental, condemning. May get 'satisfaction' but can never know joy. May get victory over others but has no victory over the self. Stubborn, worrying, afraid, malicious. Victimhood, misery, apathy. Win or lose, not win-win. Will violate the rights of others. Poorer health, addiction problems. Operates on emergency emotions (jealousy, hostility, self-pity, fear, anxiety). Limited comprehension, dominated by Lower Mind. Materialistic, possessive.

Below LoC 200 Notes (Based on Hawkins' books):

1. At the time of Buddha (536-480 BC) the level of consciousness (LoC) for mankind was about 90. By the time of Christ, the overall average LoC for mankind was about 100, still far below the important LoC 200 threshold.
2. Over the next 1000 years the overall LoC for mankind rose to about 150-180. From the 1930s to about the early 1980s mankind's LoC was about 185.
3. From the late 1980s until about 2004 the overall LoC for mankind was about 205.
4 But don't forget, these are averages, only. A staggering 85% of mankind still calibrates below LoC 200. The reason the average is higher than LoC 200 is that, for example, according to Hawkins, one individual at LoC 500 counterbalances 750,000 individuals below LoC 200, and so on, because the MoC is a logarithmic scale. Therefore, the 15% of the world's population above LoC 200 more than counterbalances the 85% below LoC 200.
5. Below LoC 200, the primary motivation is physical survival, meaning it's ProtoEgo driven.

200 to 250 200 Is a critical threshold from force to power Integrity arises Anabolic		Cross-over at 200 from catabolic state (below 200) to anabolic state of the beginning of consciousness and power. From 200 upwards, the person begins to be motivated by courage, begins to see better outcomes as feasible. This courage enables them to move forward. They begin to practise trust. Capacity for awareness and maturity arises.	Takes rigid stances. Materialistic, possessive, aggressive.

The levels of hope		Life has risen above brute survival.	

LoC 200-250 Notes:

1. It is a life-changing event for people to pass into LoC 200 and higher. It is transformational for their lives, if they can maintain it. They may be at LoC 200 or higher in some aspects of their life but still be below LoC 200 in other aspects of their life; and it will wax and wane, depending on the issue they're dealing with.
2. This LoC 200-250 breakthrough signifies a shift from Low Mind (ProtoEgo) survival existence to above Low Mind.
3. LoC 200 is the crucial level of change from catabolic (destructive of life) to anabolic (supportive of life).

310 to 399 Anabolic, but not yet rationally minded		From LoC 310 people begin to experience willingness and intention/motivation. At these levels of consciousness people are willing to forgive themselves as well as others and look for harmony in life. Non-intellectual. The rationality of the 400s has not yet been attained.	Still materialistic.
400 to 499 Anabolic, but entering a danger zone Dualistic Blinded by intellectual ego, vanity False piety The intellectual ego Is hypnotised and	8% of humankind	At these levels, reason and intellect are given great sway over one's life. Education/learning are viewed as vital. Entrepreneurism can flourish. This is the level of duality (conceptualised by 'this and that', 'here and there', 'you and me', 'them and us', 'then and now', etc). This is limitation of context called paradigm blindness.	Linear intellectual logic and reasoning doesn't ask the valid questions. Gets 'correct' but invalid answers. Humanistic (a symptom of anthropocentric egotism). LoC 400 to 499 is a breeding ground for intellectual vanity and even atheism (spiritual denial) which calibrates at the same low level as scepticism and cynicism (160-180) because it signifies negative pre-judgment rather than true inquiry with an open, honest, unbiased mind. Erroneously believes that linear logic/reason leads to truth. Wrongly believes that nothing is real unless it is quantifiable using linear logic and 'proof'. Hamstrung by Newtonian concepts of causality (only LoC 460) A → B → C,

seduced by the vanity of intellect False wisdom The ego Is at its highest and humility at its lowest			which actually defines the world of force (not power). Materialistic.

LoC 400-499 Notes:

To get beyond the ego vanity and ego tyranny of ego intellect at levels 400 to 499 – where 'logic' and 'reason' are cast in the role as the arbiters of 'reality' and truth – one has to realise that the duality model of Newtonian reasoning is actually contrived and wrong. Most people cannot make this leap of consciousness due to their intellectual ego. Even Einstein couldn't manage it.

500 to 599 (500 Is the crucial cross-over from duality) Early spiritual status Ego being seriously challeng ed	4% Of humankind	The linear, restricted reason of the 400s is superseded in favour of truth (that is, validity rather than correctness). Visionary. At 500, Love (large 'L') and altruism begin to emerge. At 540, unconditional Love is a primary motivating force and this brings inner joy. Material possessions become less relevant	

LoC 500-599 Notes:

1. The Love (big 'L') referred to at MoC 500 and beyond is ego-less. It is not the worldly ego-full love (characterised by intense emotions combining physical attraction, physical passion, possessiveness, jealousy, the desire to control or 'own' and eroticism). Whereas worldly love is one-on-one, waxes and wanes depending on the conditions, the MoC level 500 Love is unconditional, unchanging and permanent and is not limited to, say, your family, is not on-one-one.

600 to 699 Anabolic	Only one person in many tens of millions	At LoC 600, 'enlightenment' begins. God consciousness has emerged. Inner peace. Individuals at this level often remove themselves from the world. Non-materialistic. Ordinary carnal motivations are dissolving. Illnesses, diseases sometimes have a tendency to heal.	No known ego 'weaknesses'
700 to 999 Ego-less? (Ego has become E-gone?)		From LoC 700, enlightenment increases exponentially. The salvation of humanity becomes a motivating factor for one's life.	No known ego 'weaknesses'
1000		Fully ethereal mind, in the context of the physical human form.	No known ego 'weaknesses'.

Negative Motivations and Attitudes...

You need to avoid negative motivations and attitudes because whatever is negative (below LoC 200 on the MoC) is ego-centric, is based on force (not on power) and will trigger counterforce from other ego-driven people.

You Have Choice...

You, like every other human who has ever lived or will live, regardless of circumstances, is given the power of choice, as a birth right. So, it is you – not fate, not some invisible hand – that elects to use power or force in your life.

The higher your motivations, attitudes and qualities the more freedom you will have from your ProtoEgo, and the more freedom you will have from negative outcomes in your life.

According to Hawkins (*Truth vs Falsehood*, p 235) above MoC level 540 freedom is a constant in your life. If he's correct (and I don't believe he is) it means you need to understand what motivations, attitudes and qualities operate at MoC level 540 so that they become your goal.

IQ Isn't an Issue...

You don't need a high IQ to be successful in life. By successful I mean you are genuinely at peace and enjoying life and you are a living resource for others. I don't mean you're an unhappy, despondent billionaire.

Ego Is Low Mind and Is Therefore Dangerous...

Pivotal to your ability to engage positive rather than negative motivations, attitudes and qualities is your ego and your attitudes. So you need to understand your ego.

Your ego, like mine and everyone else's is opinionated, biased, presumptuous, vain and selfish.

The main problem with ego is that it is based on attitudes of force (below LoC 200 on Hawkins' MoC). Ego sees and measures your life – who you are and who you can become – in terms of material possessions, reputation, the esteem of others, your trophies and your worldly desires. There's no room for what Hawkins refers to as your higher mind to develop when your ego is in control.

Insight: With your ego in control, you'll battle to break through the MoC threshold level of LoC 200 and having failed to do so your life cannot be one of fulfilment or peace.

The Two Key Levels of the MoC... LoC 200 and LoC 500...

As discussed, the MoC level 200 is the crossover from ego-driven low mind (force) to higher mind (power).

But it's not necessarily a crossover to lesser ego. In fact it can give rise to new ego problems. Many people get stuck in the LoC 400s due to the emergence of intellectual ego. This trap has snared even the intellectually gifted such as Sir Isaac Newton, Albert Einstein and Stephen Hawking; all of whom calibrate at MoC level 499, according to David Hawkins.

Using Hawkins' MoC as a scale, why is it that the step from LoC 499 to LoC 500 is so great? The answer lies in what the 400s signify. They are a huge improvement on LoC 199, because they have harnessed some, but not all, of the power available above LoC 200. After all, according to Hawkins the levels of consciousness go to infinity. For example, he calibrated the apostles at 990, Jesus and Buddha at 1000, (*Reality, Spirituality, and Modern Man*, p116) and Archangels at 50,000 (*Truth vs Falsehood*, p383).

So, what goes on in the LoC 400s that makes those levels problematical? The answer is that although the 400s are the levels of reason and the intellect they are nonetheless levels of consciousness that are still hamstrung (probably even more hamstrung) by the ego.

Insight: Hawkins says that on his MoC level LoC 500 is the level of 'love', and that unconditional love begins at level LoC 540 (*Truth vs Falsehood*, p xxv); but you have to be careful with how you interpret the word love in the context of the MoC; as Dr Hawkins explains in *Power vs Force*, (p 111-113). For more on this, refer to Chapter 12 of this book, which discusses your ego's view of love.

Duality and Causality V Truth... The Problem of the LoC 400s...

Hawkins' consciousness level LoC 400 is all about intelligence and reason. Once people reach this level, which is not difficult, they can use their reason to identify and evaluate large amounts of data (such as is done every day in the sciences, law, engineering, and so on).

The drawback with the levels of reason is that although they herald the awakening of the intellect – which is a positive shift – they are based on the duality of Newtonian physics which is linear based on differential equations which lead to approximations, but not to truth, not to essence. Many people who have been educated in the sciences tend to treat it as infallible, when it is nothing of the kind. They seem to feel that they need to be able to explain the universe in order to feel secure. This attitude is one of vanity, with its seat in their ego.

Key Lessons from the MoC...

There are several key points that potentially follow from Dr Hawkins' MoC, for the purpose of this book, namely:

- we all have a consciousness starting point, and they aren't the same for everyone
- choice is the catalyst, and we all have freedom of choice
- motivation and intention will impact on the choices you make

- the ultimate goal is to elicit truth from all our endeavours because the more truth we have the higher our level of consciousness and the greater our freedom.

So, we now need to look at these, briefly, before we continue.

On Hawkins' MoC, What's Your LoC Starting Point…?

According to Hawkins (*Truth vs Falsehood*, p xxiv), each of us was attuned to a specific level of consciousness by virtue of a combination of inherited propensity plus the consequence of the choices we make over long periods of time.

According to Dr Hawkins, this doesn't mean that your life is determined by fate; it means that we tend to start at the point where our forbears' choices put us at the time we were born. It means nothing more than our family history, like our State's or country's history, impacts on things.

Most importantly, it's your choices that determine where you will be at various stages of your life and where you will finish.

Each of us is gifted with the option of choice and by our own hand we determine our own fate. According to Hawkins (*Truth v Falsehood*, p 233) we are free to the same degree that we are 'enlightened' (whatever 'enlightened' means). So, Hawkins would say you should make choices that are based on the higher levels of the MoC. For example, choose who your peer groups are; and steer clear of sceptics and cynics. Remember, according to Hawkins, the sceptics and cynics calibrate below LoC 200 (at LoC 160), because they reflect negative pre-judgment.

Insight: Atheists are sceptics.

The sceptics are poisonous to you because at LoC 160 their views on the point in question do not reflect true enquiry with an open mind; and their attitude, their motivation, on the point is catabolic (destructive of life).

If you won't make the brave, valid, choices you will remain stuck in your current quagmire; it's that simple.

What's Your Current Level of Motivation and Intention (LoC 310)...?

To make something happen, such as a change to your life's circumstances or outcomes requires motivation; and it has to be a different motivation than that which has got you where you currently are, if you're not where you want to be.

You will get results and outcomes based on that which you emanate; be it low level force or higher-level power. The higher your motivations (by reference to the attitudes and behaviours on the MoC) the more you will progress to satisfactory outcomes in your life.

'Success' is the automatic emergent from, or by-product of, constructive intention and behaviour.

What Is Truth...?

According to Hawkins (*Truth vs Falsehood*, p 49) truth is not only a product of content and context but is also critically related to one's specific level of consciousness:

"Each level of consciousness results in a definition of truth that is concordant to that specific level, together with its own language and qualifications that fit its culture and time" (*Truth vs Falsehood*, p 13).

The higher the motivation or intention is on the MoC, the more truthful the act or omission or conduct is.

Be careful listening to advice from people you believe are in the LoC 400-499 range, especially if their views are sceptical. Intellectual scepticism is a virulent disease and the virus at the heart of it is blind, vain, know-it-all ego. Treat them with caution. You can expect them to have their 'facts' but don't expect them to have truth or wisdom. You won't find wisdom in the LoC 400-499 range, because they are the levels of ego intellect.

As René Descartes (1596-1650) pointed out, such people cannot differentiate seeming appearance from what actually is; they cannot distinguish between their mind's own projections and true reality. They have blind faith in their intellect; which means they have blind faith in their ego.

The MoC Isn't a Layer Cake... It's Really Another Ego Spiral...

In my view, one of the unfortunate, from my perspective, aspects of Hawkins' MoC is that it's depicted as a layer cake; whereas a better picture might be given if it were depicted as a spiral; such as is the case with the various levels of Clare Graves' Spiral Dynamics model; because the MoC works on the same principle in my view; and both the spirals are actually products of ego.

Snakes and Ladders Spirals...

Just as you can move up, and down, the Spiral Dynamics spiral – or you may be at different levels of the Spiral depending on the particular aspect of your life you're dealing with – the same is true of the MoC, in my belief.

Each choice you make will calibrate at a particular LoC. That level will depend on your motivation, attitude and intention – and level of ego. Hawkins gives a good example of this in the case of the English molecular biologist, Francis Crick (1916-2004). Crick apparently referred to himself as a humanist; which is typical of people in the LoC ranges 400-499 of the MoC.

Crick said that human problems can and must be faced in terms of human moral and intellectual resources without involving supernatural authority. He apparently advocated that humanism should replace religion as a guiding force for humanity.

Crick referred to religion as being comprised of fables. He was plainly an atheist (and a sceptic). He pre-judged the question of whether or not God exists, based on his intellectual vanity and hubris.

Hubris (Force) V Humility (Power)...

Hawkins' team calibrated Crick (*Power vs Force*, pp 86-87) for his research that led to the discovery of the double helix pattern of DNA, and the score was LoC 440. They then tested Crick's last research, which was intended by Crick to prove that human consciousness is merely a product of neuronal activity of the human brain, and the score was a dismal LoC 135; indicating that Crick, by his own research, had actually shown that human consciousness is *not* merely a result of neuronal brain activity.

Crick's problem – which is a common and very serious issue for people in the LoC levels 400 to 499 – was ego and vanity. He was no doubt an intellectually clever man; but his ego built itself a pedestal and placed itself on it. In that sense, he was no different than millions of others before him, going all the way back to Nimrod. Crick plainly lacked a vital prerequisite for gaining *real* knowledge, and indeed wisdom; and that prerequisite is humility (that is, lack of ego). You cannot have a big ego and be humble at the same time, so choose the latter.

Insight: The antidote for ego is humility; and humility is of the heart, not of the mind.

Insight: If you're stuck in the no-man's land of LoC 400-499, you're at serious risk of falling back below LoC 200 in countless of your choices, because of your ego; just as Francis Crick did.

For This Journey Heart Is More Important Than Mind...

From the perspective of Hawkins' MoC, whereas LoC 200 is a vital cross-over point between Lower Mind physical survival and the dawn of hope (that comes at LoC 200), the LoC 400s are a no-man's land where your intellectual ego struggles to stay in control at all costs; and it cannot do that if you reach and remain at or above LoC 500.

The only way you can counter your ego is with the innate wisdom of your heart, once you have crossed the LoC 200 threshold. The heart can never really be fooled; it can only be shut out or shouted down by the ego mind.

Light cannot enter a closed box, as Dr Hawkins put it (*Power vs Force*, p 266).

The point is that the ego, like force, is self-serving (selfish), and repels, whereas the heart has innate power and seeks to serve others. To the unbridled ego the end always justifies the means. Your ego will sell out truth for expediency, every time.

Insight: If you let it, your ego will put a ceiling on your evolution of consciousness/ awareness. It will block your path to growth and freedom. It did it to Francis Crick, Albert Einstein, Sir Isaac Newton and René Descartes; and it can do it to you – but only if you let it. Don't let it.

Your Ego and What the 'Facts' Mean...

Even if there is agreement about the data or 'facts', and even if there's agreement about how to define truth there will, yet, be endless disagreement about what it 'means' or signifies. This dilemma is called 'hermeneutics'. It's a symptom of the reality that mankind doesn't know the facts let alone the truth; and that's because we're searching with our ego.

What's the Question, Anyhow...?

Mankind's dilemma is compounded by the fact that we often have to resort to heuristics because we can't even figure out what the right question is to trigger the enquiry to get the correct answer.

Insight: A heuristic is the process or practice that is a form of mental shortcut, a 'rule of thumb' or a guestimate, or, supposedly, 'common sense'. All your guesses or estimates or assumptions are based on heuristics.

Heuristics are fine if you're measuring the amount of wood and chicken wire you need to build a chicken coop, but don't be fooled into thinking that such an approach can be used to find universal truths; as is apparently believed by the intellectuals who are stagnating in LoC levels 400-499 on Hawkins' MoC. Their problem is that they're using the wrong tools. It reminds me of the old saying that when your only tool is a hammer every problem looks like a nail.

What You Learned in ThIs Chapter

- you can now see that although getting the wrong results or outcomes in life is common it's by no means inevitable
- it all comes down to the choices you make
- so, if we add more tools to your 'Choices Box' maybe you can start making better choices and getting better outcomes in your daily life

Chapter 6

It's Okay to Have Bungled Things, So Far...

What You'll Discover in This Chapter...

- You need to be wary of your intellect
- You can't abandon your ego – it's part of who you are – and you don't want to be at war with it, so it needs to be re-programmed for you to get better outcomes in life
- You have to be wary of your peer groups, and peer group ego, and avoid sceptics
- You have to let your heart have a say

Your Ego Doesn't Want You to Change...

Your ego thinks it's your best friend, your staunchest ally, and the only one smart enough to ensure that this mean world doesn't devour you.

This is because your ego is a hindbrain or ProtoBrain survival version of you. In many ways your ego's job has become redundant, because, unlike your stone age ancestors, you're a lot safer from the ancient threats your ego had to watch out for; but your ego doesn't like the thought that it has become obsolete.

All the things I said earlier in this book about your subconscious being paranoid, obsessive, compulsive and myopic actually refer to your ego.

It's your ego that is currently delivering to you the unsatisfactory outcomes in life that you're trying to change; but that's no reason to treat your ego as your enemy – and it would be a mistake to do so. Going to war with your ego will actually make things worse rather than better, so don't do it.

To succeed with this transition, you have to evolve your consciousness, your awareness, but as far as your ego is concerned, you're doing just fine so it doesn't want to evolve.

You need to evolve your ProtoEgo, but the worst thing you could do would be to accuse and condemn it. You mustn't try to eliminate it by attacking it with negative self-judgments, guilt, or remorse over lost opportunities.

If you attack your ego, it will tenaciously resist and it has the immense energy of your subconscious signature filtering and behavioural programmes to back it up.

Your Ego Feeds off Negative Energy...

Your ego, like mine, feeds off pain, suffering, guilt, having the need to always be 'right', and feeling that it's a victim, or even a martyr. In fact, your ego is addicted to these perceptions or feelings.

Ego and the MoC...

If we look at ego from the perspective of David Hawkins' Map of Consciousness ('MoC') we can see that all of the ego's tools for dealing with life's challenges are from below LoC 200, which means they're all based on force, not power. This is so whether its tools are emotional, intellectual or physical.

Force Causes Counterforce...

The greatest shortcoming of all the tools of force is that they produce counter-force. On the other hand, power does not have counter-power; it just has ever more empowerment. This means you should use, and only use, the MoC tools that are found at LoC 200 or higher, or you will always hit hurdles in life that you cannot surmount.

Insight: Unfortunately, the MoC presented by David Hawkins doesn't give you all the tools. There are big gaps in the MoC.

A Reminder About Peer Groups... The Company You Keep...

As David Hawkins says in *Power v Force* (at page 230):

"One does not get over pessimism by associating with cynics; the popular idea that you are defined by the company you keep has some clinical basis."

Look at where your current peer groups, your current reference groups, are in life. Are they where you want to be? Are they growing as people or just repeating the same failed behaviours, over and over? To use Hawkins MoC as a scale, are they operating at a level above LoC 499? If not, they will hold you back on the journey to quell your ego and change your results and outcomes in life.

Insight: You can always ask yourself questions about your reference groups or peer groups that might shed light on them, such as:

- What do they talk about?
- What do they read?
- What are their goals in life – are they just material, just hedonistic?
- What are their values?
- Who do they look up to, admire or praise?

If the answers don't line up with where you want to be in life then why are you squandering your valuable time with them? After all, time is the most finite and valuable thing you will ever have in this life. (Psalm 39:4-5; Ephesians 5:11, 15-17; Colossians 4:5; Proverbs 14:23; Ecclesiastes 11:4).

So, What About the Atheists…?

I've said that you should avoid sceptics (including atheists) if you want to succeed in life. What I didn't say is that if you are an atheist, you will never achieve what you are capable of in your life. You might achieve a lot – materially and intellectually – but you won't reach the heights you're capable of; because the highest level an atheist will attain on the MoC, even if he or she is intellectually gifted or has a high IQ, is LoC 499.

It's true that LoC 499 was the level attained by clever people such as Sir Isaac Newton, René Descarte, Sigmund Freud and Albert Einstein; but it's still far short of where you'll find true self-awareness and truth; which is what you need in order to become the best version of you; and it's still far short of who you can become.

Let me add that Isaac Newton was not an atheist, whereas the position with Albert Einstein seems ambiguous. Einstein may have been an agnostic; a believer in a deistic god (as opposed to a personal God). On the other hand, it seems that Freud regarded God as an infantile illusion; which means he had high intellect but low true consciousness, low true self-awareness.

There are two key levels of consciousness on the MoC. The first is LoC 200, at which point people can first engage the power of consciousness. A whopping 85% of humanity has not yet attained that level according to David Hawkins (*Truth v Falsehood*, pp 90-91).

The second key level is LoC 500. This second threshold cannot be crossed by those driven by a belief in the duality and causation concepts of Newtonian linear physics; which accounts for almost all scientists, because they require linear 'proof', and linear proof is a matter of force (below LoC 200 on the MoC).

Science and philosophy seem to walk hand-in-hand with cynicism, scepticism; and, sometimes downright hostility, when it comes to God. Examples of scientists and intellectuals who vehemently deny God are Sigmund Freud, Francis Crick, Stephen Hawking, Richard Dawkins (*The God Delusion*) and Yuval Harari (*Homo Deus, A Brief History of Tomorrow*).

Insight: True consciousness and self-awareness are in reality non-intellectual (of the heart, spiritual), so if you deny the spiritual you are doomed to the mediocrity of intellectualism.

Francis Crick... Another Lost Intellectual...

In his research, Hawkins reports that he tested tens of thousands of concepts and people. He found that scepticism (which includes intellectual cynicism or intellectual bias) calibrates at only LoC 160 on the MoC, because it reflects negative prejudgment.

As an example, he refers to the famous British professor, Francis Crick (*Power vs Force*, pp 86-87) and the pitfalls of intellectual vanity. He notes that Crick's research into DNA calibrated at LoC 440. However, Crick's later research, by which Crick intended to prove that consciousness is merely a product of neuronal activity, calibrated at only LoC 135 (untruth); meaning his theory on consciousness is completely false, because it's below LoC 200.

As Dr Hawkins noted, the propensity of many intellectuals (such as Crick, Dawkins and Harari) to deny spiritual reality relegates them to LoC 499 (at best); and even below 200 when it comes to the subject of self-awareness, true conscious and the truth about creation.

The Heart, not the Mind, Is Where Wisdom Resides...

The problem with intellect (intellectual ego) as your sole or main compass in life is that it's easily misled, beguiled, seduced and fooled, and there are plenty of celebrity, self-appointed, wise men (such as Richard Dawkins, Yuval Harari and Francis Crick) whose vanity or doubtful or misguided motives or agendas (such as humanism or anthropocentrism) will lead you in the wrong direction.

In *Truth v Falsehood*, (p134-135) Hawkins comes up with some fascinating MoC calibrations for intellectual stuff, for example:

Current Science/Theory/Concept	MoC Level ('true' only at or below thIs LoC)	Absolutely True	Absolutely False
Big Bang source of the Universe theory			√
Divinity as source of the Universe		√	
Darwinian theory of evolution	450		
Intelligent design	480		
Earth warming due to man's pollution (that is, anthropogenic global warming)			√
'Greenhouse' gas earth warming theory (anthropogenic global warming)			√
Newtonian duality and causality principles	460		
Parallel Universe theory			√
Telekinesis		√	
Water on Mars		√	
Current principles of Clinical Kinesiology	600		
Atheistic ideology			√
Atheism	165		
Anti-religion/God	135-180		
Existence of extra-terrestrials			√
Existence of UFOs			√
Jesus and Mary were married			√
Jesus' descendants became French rulers			√
There is a hidden Bible code			√
Reincarnation as lesser species			√
Science generally	450-460		
Theology (as opposed to spiritual truth)	460		

As Dr Hawkins puts it (*Power vs Force*, p176):

"Although the intellect is easily fooled, the heart recognises the truth. Where the intellect is limited, the heart is unlimited; where the intellect is intrigued by the temporary, the heart is only concerned with the permanent."

Unfortunately, for the intellectually vain, for those who are cynical towards anything their intellectual hubris will not countenance, it's a case of light (truth) not being able to enter a closed box (their heads).

"There is nothing the mind [that is, intellect] believes that is not fallacious at a higher level of awareness... The mind [that is, intellect] does not even experience the world, but only sensory reports of it." (*Power vs Force*, p266).

The Example of Medicine V Healing...

A great example of intellect (limited consciousness) versus heart (or epiconsciousness, that is understanding beyond intellect) is holistic medicine.

Traditional science-based (intellect-based) western medicine (what homeopaths often refer to as 'allopathic' medicine) relies only on mechanical, electrical and chemical approaches *to treat conditions*. On the other hand, holistic approaches, that come from human consciousness (that is, heart) rather than human intellect, emphasise *healing* rather than merely *treating*.

Science-based western medicine follows the Newtonian physics approach; which is linear, based on the limited concepts of duality and causation. So, at best, science-based western medicine will try to influence protoplasm or cells. On the other hand, holistic medicine is aimed at influencing the energy field that surrounds and affects the human body.

The 12 Steps...

Another great example of heart trumping intellect is the well-known and accepted 12-step self-help movement, which has shown beyond doubt the capacity of consciousness (the heart) to heal. The first among these groups was, of course, Alcoholics Anonymous. At the heart of the 12-Step systems is what equates to a transition to a higher level of consciousness on Hawkins' MoC.

So, don't treat this challenge of transition to a better you as an intellectual challenge; or you'll only get part of the way there. Try to see it as a journey you will make with your heart; a journey to higher levels of consciousness; rather than a journey of acquiring data or knowledge as we are traditionally taught to do.

What You Learned in This Chapter...

- Peer groups are made up of people and if those people are below LoC 500 their egos are in control of their motivations, intentions and choices, and that may be counter-productive for you
- You will end up in life where *your* motivations, *your* intentions and *your* choices direct you
- Intellect is a two-edged sword
- Evolving, epi-consciously, is not an exercise of intellect
- Unfortunately Hawkins didn't really deal with the heart on his MoC – I know this because the heart operates from a base of humility and humility isn't even mentioned on the MoC

Chapter 7
Beware False Flags...

What You'll Discover in This Chapter...

- A lot people have written a lot of stuff that can be loosely described as self-help or empowering but most of it won't help you, and I'll refer to a couple of these books in this chapter
- There are also many well-written books from which you can truly benefit, and I'll give you a short list of them in this chapter

Let's Look at a Couple of the Unhelpful Books...

I could have picked quite a few books that I have read that won't help you, but I've opted for *The Subtle Art of Not Giving a F*ck* and *The Secret*. So, let's get into them and out of them as soon as we can.

The Subtle Art of Not Giving a F*ck by Mark Mason (2016, Harper Collins) is an example of shallow pop psychology. In my view, it has nothing of value to offer anyone. In summary, what Mason says is:

- His book supposedly helps you think more clearly about what you're choosing to find important in your life and what you're choosing to find unimportant
- We suffer in life because it's biologically useful to do so
- Decision making based on how you feel, or 'emotional intuition', without the aid of reason 'sucks'
- Our values determine the nature of our problems
- We're really just apes and because of this we instinctively measure ourselves against others and vie for status

Need I say more! This is meaningless pop psychology wrapped up in a trashy title. If you've read Mason's book and believe you got value, you're not yet ready for this book.

The Secret is a best seller of 2006, written by Rhonda Byrne and apparently inspired by earlier self-help notions espoused by a Russian occultist Madame Blavatsky (1831-1891) and Norman Vincent Peale (1898-1993).

The premise of this line of self-help ideas is that merely thinking about certain things will make them appear in your life. Without me going any further you should realise that such ideas are dubious. If you don't believe me, just think about winning the lottery, buy a ticket, and see how far you get.

It's annoying enough that such snake-oil ideas keep getting trotted out to gullible readers but what makes *The Secret* far worse, in my view, is the author's sloppy, self-serving, or misguided reference to Christian scripture, to try to give credence to her concept. Byrne, either ignorantly or brazenly, distorts the meaning of Matthew 21:22.

"And whatever things you ask in prayer, believing, you will receive." (New Spirit Filled Life Bible, 2002, Thomas Nelson, Inc).

"And everything that you shall ask in prayer, believing, you should receive." (The Holy Bible in its Original Order, A New English Translation, 2007, York Publishing Company, Hollister, California).

The primary problems I have with Byrne's use of this scriptural citation are:

- It refers to 'prayer', and in the Christian context prayer has very specific elements or pre-requisites that are based on spiritual acceptance of God and Christ
- In Christianity, Christ is the one and only Gateway for prayer and for spiritual salvation – not a conduit for material earthly wealth, as Byrne suggests
- To access the Gateway, you have to repent and be baptised – properly baptised by full immersion under water – and you cannot repent and cannot be baptised unless and until you are mature enough to, are willing to, and intend to, understand and accept God and Christ

Leaving aside Byrne's mis-application of scripture, my view is that her book has nothing of value to offer you. Don't bother with *The Secret* if you want to get ahead in life. The idea that you can simply wish things into your life is fanciful.

Your Heart Is Your Key...

In *The Art of War*, written in about the 5th century BC, attributed to a Chinse military strategist, Sun Tzu, the author says:

"Victorious warriors win first and then go to war, while defeated warriors go to war first and then seek to win."

What Sun Tzu meant, in my view, is that any challenge in life must be 'won' within you before you can bring it to reality. In other words, you must not only *think* it, you must also *believe* it (in your heart, not just your mind) and you must *emote* it. To emote something means to *feel* that you have already achieved that goal.

Insight: The key process is the emoting, which is preceded by the thinking and the believing. The emoting is essential because it engages the power of your heart which engages the power of your survival brain, your ProtoBrain. For as long as your conscious mind, heart and subconscious mind are attuned in this way you are unstoppable. So, don't accept the simplistic erroneous advice of books such as *The Secret*.

Insight: Your heart has a conscience and is inherently truthful so if you twist it to ego-driven unconscionable behaviour you will suffer internal conflict and sickness.

The Heart Does Not Know Fear...

Whereas your subconscious mind knows fear, your heart does not when it comes to things of good conscience. Your heart instinctively knows truth which means it is attuned to power, not merely to force, and it is fearless; but the power of the heart is on a much higher level than the power referred to in Hawkins' MoC. Once you truthfully engage your heart in the thinking, believing and emoting process you empower yourself on a spiritual level. Your heart can guide your mind if you allow it to, but that means reaching a heart-centred level of consciousness.

To Your Subconscious Mind the Unknown Equates to Fear...

Your subconscious mind wants you to survive and for that reason it has a natural preference for the familiar over the unfamiliar; even when the familiar is not giving you the outcomes in life you are trying to achieve. This is why your comfort zones must be acknowledged and understood for what they are.

Fear Is Your one and only True Enemy...

If there is one overarching emotion in life that is more catabolic (life destroying) than any other it's fear.

Insight: Your ego lives in fear but a heart of good conscience is fearless.

Master your fears and you can transform your life; and you surely realise that just *thinking* your way to a life of fulfilment, as suggested by the book *The Secret*, is fanciful. What is required is that you overcome:

- Your self-imposed fears
- Your self-imposed comfort zone upper limits
- Your learned (socially engineered) ineffective attitudes and behaviours
- Your negative dispositions, meaning any feeling or attitude below LoC 200 (courage) on David Hawkins' Map of Consciousness
- Your ego

It means replacing all this negativity with anabolic (life enhancing) attitudes, beliefs and behaviours. This means, for starters, that you'll have to reach LoC 310, the level of willingness and intention. You have to then implement the practices, the behaviours, that will transform you, using your heart.

Don't Let Intellect Hold You Back...

Be on your guard for the sceptical peer groups and authors who do not have faith in your journey; they can't even comprehend it. They don't have the heart it takes to walk this path. All they have is ignorance and ego or intellectual vanity and ego.

You will know them by their fruits (Matthew 7:15-20). They are like the false prophets that Jesus spoke of (Matthew 24:11). You must do something these cynics and non-believers cannot do: engage your heart.

Helpful Books...

Let's look at a short list of books that I do recommend. In the case of David Hawkins' books, however, beware of the shortcomings I have identified on his MoC and his comments on Christian scripture.

Dr David Hawkins	• *Power vs Force* • *Truth vs Falsehood* • *Reality, Spirituality and Modern Man* • *Healing and Recovery* • *Discovery of The Presence of God* • *The Eye of the I* • *Transcending the Levels of Consciousness*
Bruce H. Lipton	• *The Biology of Belief*
Joe Dispenza	• *Evolve Your Brain, The Science of Changing Your Mind*
Gay Hendricks	• *The Big Leap*
Dr Wayne Dyer	• *The Power of Intention, Learning to Co-create Your World Your Way*

Assessing Books... My Simple Test...

So, how can you tell if a non-fiction book (which are the only books I read) are worth the paper they're written on? Well, below is a simple ten-point assessment test that I created to help me rank books.

Kevin Staffa's Five-Stage Book Assessment
(for Non-fiction Books)
(Maximum score Is 10 – max of 2 for each category)

Date: _____ / _____ / 20_____

Title   of   Book: _____   **Author:**

_____

		Choose One Score
1	**First: (integrity)** For true enquiry with an open honest mind, devoid of negative pre-judgment (devoid of scepticism and cynicism) and for not misrepresenting opposing points of view Maximum 2 points	2 1 0
2	**Second: (objectivity)** For rigorous, detailed investigation of the subject matter Maximum: 2 points	2 1 0
3	**Third: (methodology/scholarship)** For transparently sound methodology, that others can test or audit as opposed to supposition, and for clear explanation/writing style Maximum: 2 points	2 1 0
4	**Fourth: (originality)** For originality/for leading the way Maximum: 2 points	2 1 0
5	**Fifth: (legacy)** For legacy value – for creating something we can benefit from right now and build on Maximum: 2 points	2 1 0
	MAXIMUM 10 POINTS TOTAL	

What You Learned in This Chapter...

- You should read, read, read – but don't waste your time with snake-oil, pop psychology garbage
- Look beyond your mind to your heart if you want to find truth because your heart will ask different questions than your ego
- There is plenty of well-written material that will help you on this journey, and the choice is yours as to whether you will use it
- False guides (and their egos) are as dangerous as the wrong peer groups, so you have to think and choose with your heart not just your mind

Chapter 8
Your Ego and Spiritual Evolution...

What You'll Discover in This Chapter...

- Many scientists and other intellectuals have (their intellectual egos have) declared that there's no creator, that you're just a biological machine with no meaning or purpose for your life
- However, as we will see in Chapter 9, there's been a spiritual consciousness unfolding for some time and if you're not part of it you'll miss out on the biggest opportunity of your lifetime – and you won't be part of it if your ego has its way
- The only real barrier between you and the ultimate things you can achieve in your life is your ego, in its various manifestations – including your troublesome spiritual ego
- Egos are often found in gangs of bullies masquerading as integrous groups that purport to have the interests and welfare of others at the forefront of their minds when in truth their motives are narcissistic if not sinister
- You shouldn't let 'things' get in your way

The Ego's Linear World View V the Non-Linear Reality of Creation...

The linear world of duality and causality, which is the invention of man's intellectual ego, is one that takes for granted that human logic, human reason (that is, intellect) can and does lead to the discovery of universal reality and universal truth and can deliver universal peace and abundance.

This linear world theory, as a concept of mathematics and physics, is attributed to the English mathematician, physicist, astronomer and theologian, Sir Isaac Newton (1643-1727). In effect, the Newtonian physics paradigm proffers a scientific view, or and intellectual ego view, of reality.

This Newtonian concept of linear reality is based on the scientific belief in two concepts:

- First, there's 'duality' – it's based on the scientific belief that in the universe there is a separation of 'things', namely 'this' and 'that', 'here' and 'there', 'then' and 'now' and 'you' and 'me', and so on
- Secondly, there's 'causality' – the scientific belief in what is termed a deterministic *linear* sequence, where A causes B which then causes C

Frankly, I don't care whether, on a daily basis, we think in terms of 'things' or not. However, I am concerned about not having my potential for spiritual awareness curtailed by my ego's intellectual inventions, biases and beliefs.

This Newtonian duality and causality model is, of course, nothing more than a belief, a perception. It might be proclaimed to be undeniable scientific fact; but it's not based on laws of the universe and it's not how, or only how, the universe works. It's based on the flimsy basis of man's experience and man's logic.

There's Also a Non-Duality, Non-Linear Reality...

Nowadays, due to the emergence of quantum mathematics, physics and mechanics many scientists believe that Newton's version of reality is actually only of limited application; meaning it's only true in certain circumstances, or at certain moments, or from time to time. This is so because our scientists, or some of them, now believe that Newtonian physics isn't consistent with the concept of the universe being holographic, as described by those such as the American physicist David Bohm (1917-1992).

What Bohm said, in effect, was that the 'Cartesian' (named after René Descartes, 1596-1650) presumption that there exist two kinds of substance, mental and physical (that is, duality) that somehow interact (that is causality) is too limited, and can be misleading.

The German physicist Werner Heisenberg (1901-1976) was another who didn't accept the clockwork universe theory of Newton; a universe where 'things' exist separately (that is, duality) and these separate 'things' follow clear laws on how to move (that is, causality); a universe where prediction is easy if you know the starting conditions.

Heisenberg, who was one of the pioneers of quantum mechanics, said we cannot measure the position (x) and the momentum (p) of a particle with absolute precision because the more accurately we know one of these values the less accurately we will know the other. This is now referred to as the ' Heisenberg uncertainty principle'.

What this means is that, because of the work of the likes of Heisenberg, many scientists now believe that the long-accepted science of conjugate variables, or the science of complementarity, isn't reliable. Examples of conjugate variables are:

- Position and momentum – the example Heisenberg referred to, above
- Time and energy (frequency)
- Entanglement and coherence
- Wave and particle related properties

Many physicists now believe that none of the above 'pairs' can be measured simultaneously, despite what earlier scientists had maintained since Newton's time. The quandary for science is that it seems that everything in the universe behaves as both a particle and as a wave at the same time. In other words, the belief in the duality of 'things' isn't necessarily sound. This means no one really knows how the universe works.

Insight: Our current science leads us to believe that a particle exists in a single place at any given instant in time and that waves are disturbances spread out in space, like ripples on a pond. So, because every 'thing' apparently behaves as both a particle and a wave at the same time, a 'thing' isn't really a thing, because it's capable of manifesting, and being described as manifesting, as both a particle and a wave at the same time.

Poincaré Got it... Up to a Point...

In fact, as early as the late 1800s, the Frenchman, Jules-Henri Poincaré, noted that the Newtonian physics of duality and causality was only mathematically accurate if the interaction under study was limited to two bodies (that is, limited to two 'things'). He noted that the introduction of a third element (a third 'thing') made Newton's equations unreliable; giving, at best, only approximations.

Are There Really any 'Things'...? Quantum Mechanics and the Superposition Principle...

The superposition principle (more a belief than a principle) of quantum mechanics states that if we have a particle that could be in several states at the same time and we can't tell which state it is actually in then it's in all those states at the same time.

According to our current science, this means that when we have our backs turned 'things' behave differently than when we are watching them (the so-called 'observer effect').

But that's not the end of the conundrum.

What About the EPR Paradox...?

In contrast, the EPR paradox says that the superposition principle of quantum mechanics is wrong because for it to be correct particles would need to be able to communicate with each other and they would have to do this faster than the speed of light; which Einstein said is impossible, and Einstein was really smart so we should all believe what he said. It would follow from this that quantum mechanics is an erroneous concept because of Einstein's beliefs. But that's still not the end of it.

Bell's Theorem...

Bell's theorem is named after John Stewart Bell (1928-1990) a quantum physicist from Northern Ireland who turned the EPR paradox idea on its head when he came up with a theoretical experiment which would give different results depending on whether particles can or cannot communicate faster than the speed of light.

But we all had to hold our breath because it took 15 years before the equipment existed that could be used to put Bell's theoretical experiment into practice. When they got all the bits together the result of the experiment was to show that entangled photons do, indeed, communicate faster than the speed of light; meaning that quantum mechanics was not done with, yet. But, of course, that doesn't mean that quantum mechanics is valid.

Insight: A photon is the smallest particle representing a quantum of light or other electromagnetic radiation. It's a bundle of electromagnetic energy, which is the source of all light. It's believed, at present, that photons are not made up of smaller particles. Entangled photons are pairs or groups of particles that generate or interact or share spatial proximity in ways such that the quantum state of each particle cannot be described independently of the state of the others.

Einstein...?

That takes us back to Einstein's theory of relativity, which is based on the premise that it's impossible for anything to travel faster than the speed of light. According to Bell's theorem, that's not true, Einstein was wrong... maybe... or maybe not... or... who knows!

Chaos Theory... And Butterflies...

This paradoxical, confused situation with man's science (man's battle between various intellectual egos) is made even more confusing due to the emergence of 'Chaos Theory', through the work of physicists such as James A. Yorke (1941-), a research professor of mathematics and physics at the University of Maryland, USA.

Chaos theory is the study of complex/dynamic systems that are extremely sensitive to (that is, dependent upon) their initial conditions; such as weather systems that are studied for the purposes of weather forecasts. It's about making *approximations*; something that, for example, meteorologists must do or they would never be able to produce weather forecasts. The problem is that the slightest change in the initial conditions can change everything else in the system. This is also referred to as the 'butterfly effect'.

So Which Science (Which Intellectual Ego) Is Right...?

Is quantum mechanics to be believed or not? The answer is that our physicists and mathematicians are still squabbling about it and we (they) don't know.

But don't go away; there's at least one alternative to quantum mechanics that allows for communicating particles but doesn't rely on the superposition principle. It's called Bohmian mechanics.

I don't intend to venture into Bohmian mechanics as I believe I have already made the point about the unreliability of intellect. So, don't allow the vain egos of the intellectual hotshots such as scientists to be your only point of reference.

I'm not disparaging science. I'm just saying don't be foolish enough to think it will ever lead to the discovery of truth or reality. It would be foolhardy to accept as unquestionably correct the determinations or predictions of the intellectual ego, no matter how forcefully the proponents of those theories might put them. For example, keep an open mind when it comes to the anthropocentric or atheistic pronouncements of the likes of Richard Dawkins, Francis Crick and Yuval Harari; and keep an open mind on theories such as the theory of the spontaneous, non-divine origin and biological evolution of mankind.

Stubborn, Anthropocentric Ego-Driven Science...

It's already been noted that, according to Dr David Hawkins, *intellectual approaches* to finding truth (such as man's science) calibrate only in the mid-400s on his MoC, and cannot, with few exceptions, pass beyond LoC 499. This is important. It's telling us that intellect doesn't equate to awareness.

According to Hawkins, most of man's science exists in the limited consciousness domain of linear content (the LoCs 400s), whereas consciousness, truth and true reality are to be found only via a consciousness that's in the non-linear domain; beyond LoC 499, assuming the MoC works on that level. In other words, unless you're living at those LoC 500+ levels, you're not going to find truth; you'll only find more scientific 'logic' and theories, and relative truth.

The intellectual egos of our scientists and other intelligentsia are a huge barrier for them, because the ego lacks consciousness. Einstein, for example, according to Dr Hawkins, calibrated at the very peak of human intellectual prowess, at LoC 499; yet he went into a scientific wilderness of sorts by rejecting the Heisenberg uncertainty principle. Einstein's mind was shut to concepts other than his own because of his intellectual ego; because his ego had to be 'right'.

Insight: Given that the greatest minds of science (Newton, Einstein, Bohm, Heisenberg, Bell, and so on) cannot agree on the basics of what the universe is this must indicate that man's intellectual ego *cannot* find truth.

Insight: Likewise, you shouldn't allow *your* intellectual ego to deceive you into dismissing the possibility of explanations of who and what you are that are at odds with the views of those such as Dawkins, Crick and Harari.

Perceived Ambit of the Current MoC Model...

In this author's view, to the extent that it's accurate, Hawkins' MoC has revealed what is merely the first tier of a consciousness *spiral* that has an infinite number of tiers; and from this first tier (which extends to, say, LoC 1000) – and possibly from none of its tiers – is it possible to pose let alone answer some of the questions Hawkins sought to answer; specifically in relation to matters such as the provenance of and validity of say Old Testament and New Testament Christian scripture; and whether, say, there is or can be reincarnation.

Insight: I believe that kinesiology being a physical phenomenon is limited to physical, anatomical tests.

One of the aspects of Hawkins' writing and his MoC that leads me to believe that although he was on the right track so far as the physical body is concerned, he was not seeing the full picture – or he was actually leaping to conclusions – is that he didn't write about, because he didn't discern, a purpose for human life on Earth (*Power vs Force*, p314); which to my mind is at the very heart of self-awareness or higher consciousness.

Without an understanding of the purpose of human life I believe he could not reliably calibrate truths that go beyond the earthly, the mundane; such as the truths that might be found in Christian scripture, including the Old Testament and the Book of Revelation.

My view is that in the case of unadulterated Christian scripture, being, as I would say it is, Divinely inspired, it is beyond the realm of testing by such primitive, earthly things as Hawkins' MoC; which after all is a creation of a man's intellect; and man's intellect is incapable of testing the Divine.

After all, Dr Hawkins believed that the LoC of Archangels was about 50,000 (*Truth vs Falsehood*, p383), so where would that put the LoC of the Creator? Plainly it would be infinity, or beyond. And given that Jesus was God the Son (part of the Elohim) (John 8:48) before he took on the role of a mortal man, for a very special purpose, His LoC was also infinite; not merely LoC 1000 as suggested by Hawkins (*Power vs Force*, p116).

Faith and Consciousness...

Plainly, the reason the Christian scripture tells us that we are required to have faith in its message is because that message is beyond the capacity of our earthly human levels of consciousness, no matter how high, to comprehend; and I believe this was deliberately made so by our Creator to ensure we undergo this test of faith. In other words, as earthly humans, we will never truly comprehend much of, if not most of, the Christian scripture, and we are not equipped to question its veracity; even with our bodies by using the kinesiological testing method. Kinesiological muscle testing just cannot do it.

When it comes to the Christian scripture, faith is trusting without proof (such as 'scientific' proof). Examples of some of the Old Testament scriptures on faith are Psalms 3:5-6, 9:10, 46:10; attributed primarily to David, the second King of the ancient Israelites; who, as a boy, slew Goliath.

Insight: God does not hide from the humble that which is needed for salvation (that is, that which is needed for us to develop faith). Jesus is recorded as having said (Matthew 11:25):

"... You have hidden these things from the wise and intelligent [those guided by ego intellect] and have revealed them to babes" [those who have trusting humble hearts that can be taught truth].

In the New Testament we are told: "For we live by faith, not by sight" (2 Corinthians 5:7, NIV); we are told not to be doubters (James 1:6, NIV). Jesus said: "Did I not tell you that if you believe you will see the glory of God?" (John 11:40, NIV).

Intellect Is Easy...

Most people, given the opportunity, can become intellectually proficient. It's not difficult. However, it seems there are very few who overcome their egos and have the sort of faith required by Christian scripture; namely, faith without 'proof'. Your ego (your fear and vanity) will keep telling you it wants proof; but spiritual consciousness, spiritual awareness, spiritual truth and spiritual reality cannot come via the conduit of man's intellect, because they are things not of the intellect. If you can accept this then you are on the launch-pad to true awakening.

Insight: Keep an open mind – meaning a mind that listens to your heart. Don't let your mind be hijacked by your ego (fear or vanity) or someone else's. If your heart is humble, you will find all the truth and wisdom you require in this earthly life.

The Strengths of the MoC...

I've said that I perceive Dr Hawkins' MoC to be far from complete. Nonetheless, I consider it to be a useful milestone in our capacity to understand ourselves to a degree; because I would say it shows that anything that's enquired into other than from a basis of humility and faith will not lead to the truth.

The MoC may be a useful tool and platform for 'enlightenment' (whatever that is); but to me this so-called enlightenment is of the intellect and is earthly and primitive.

Dr Hawkins' MoC casts some light into dark recesses; but I see his MoC as still being ego-intellect driven. Nonetheless, it may offer assistance for anyone who might want to explore say Spiral Dynamics; and the Myers-Briggs Type Indicator (MBTI).

Insight: There are 16 MBTI, each of which offers an insight into the inherent psychological preferences people seem to have. These 16 MBTI were identified by Katharine Cook Briggs (1875-1968) and her daughter Isabel Briggs Myers (1897-1980), based on the work of the Swiss psychiatrist Carl Jung (1875-1961). For example, my MBTI is INTJ. However, once again, these are largely intellectual constructs.

Insight: Whereas, according to Dr Hawkins, Sigmund Freud (1856-1939) measured only LoC 499 on the MoC, indicating that he was a prisoner of his intellectual ego, Carl Jung measured at over LoC 500; and remember, LoC 500 is, according to Dr Hawkins, the threshold that indicates a person has, as I would put it, released himself or herself from the bondage of ego intellect. In other words, Carl Jung was not blinkered by intellect to the same extent that Sigmund Freud was; so what Carl Jung says, in general, should be given more credence than what Freud says, where the two conflict; if you're using the MoC as a yardstick.

Spiral Dynamics' Change State Indicator Test and Values Profile Test...

An understanding of Spiral Dynamics is a must for anyone wanting to understand our world (historical and present), societies, human values, human failures, themselves and others; because it actually gives an insight into the ego as it operates on individual and at group levels.

The key Spiral Dynamics tests – change state indicator test and values profile test – are topics that cannot be covered in this book. Nonetheless, it's appropriate that the reader be made aware of them for self-research, as they are tools that can shed light on your various egos (ProtoEgo, intellectual ego and spiritual ego), and group egos.

Don't let your spiritual ego deceive you by masking 'theology' and 'religion' as spiritual consciousness or spiritual awareness... and don't let the MoC become your new religion...

Theology and 'religion' are the playground of your spiritual ego; and in my view Hawkins' MoC has many of the same drawbacks.

95

Just as your ego wants to hijack your intellect – by turning you into an unquestioning adherent to the theory of spontaneous, non-divine, human origin and biological evolution, and making you a humanist and an anthropocentrist – it also wants to sabotage your ventures into spiritual consciousness by foisting theology and religion onto you in the guise of them being genuine Christian spiritual consciousness. They aren't. They're fakes, imitations.

In the case of Christian scripture, if it's not exactly the same as the original it's man's 'tradition' or man's invention, and is fake. To that extent, unfortunately, Hawkins is, in my view, an imposter, an impersonator and a false prophet when he ventures into the Christian scripture with his MoC. Its uses are limited.

Whereas I keep an open mind on the veracity of the Christian scriptures based on the teachings of Jesus and the apostles there's a lot of difference between those teachings and the religious versions of Christianity foisted onto us since before the Council of Nicea (in 325 AD) convened by the Roman Emperor Constantine. These versions are sold to us primarily by the Roman Catholic Church (RCC), and to a lesser degree by the mainstream Protestant churches (Protestantism); both of which could be mistaken for worldly commercial enterprises.

As an aside, according to David Hawkins (*Truth v Falsehood*, p79) theology calibrates only in the LoCs 400s; not crossing the all-important threshold of LoC 500. I can't see how the MoC can tell anyone that; but, nonetheless, I agree.

So, if theology and religion aren't the same as the teachings of Jesus and the apostles, what are they? And if Hawkins' teachings aren't the same as those of Jesus and the apostles, what are they?

Theology is the study of theistic (God-based) beliefs. Religion refers to a set of spiritual beliefs and practices held by a theistic group, usually involving cultural traditions and rituals.

The 'religion' of the RCC and Protestantism should not, in my view, be equated to Christian spiritual truth as they are not based solely on scripture. The RCC versions are vitiated by arbitrary, convenient interpretations, and unilateral, man-made (religious ego made) changes or misinterpretations of scripture; to make them more palatable to man's ego.

The Spiritual Ego's Censorship and Re-Writing of Christian Scripture…

Below are nine examples of what I see as some of the distortions of scripture by the RCC; and bear in mind that Jesus expressly warned against

"…teaching as doctrines the commandments of men."

Jesus was warning against worship based on the law or traditions of men rather than on the word of God (Matthew 15:9; Mark 7:7; 2 John 9:11). He was saying that any such 'worship' is false worship.

First RCC distortion: The *Pope* Is my shepherd…? Peter's Church – the source of the belief that the RCC Pope has some special standing…

What the Scripture actually says: In the Old Testament only God was considered the rock upon which salvation could be founded: Psalm 27:5; Psalm 28:1.

Peter is first in the list of 12 apostles (Matthew 10:1-4, 16:13-19; Luke 6:13-16). He was often spokesman for the apostles. Peter gave the first sermon on the Pentecost (Acts 2). Peter was the apostle to the Jews. Paul was the apostle to the Gentiles. Neither one is listed as being above the other.

Peter refused homage when it was offered to him by Cornelius (Acts 10:25-28).

Peter, James and John were the three pillars in the Jerusalem Church (Galatians 2:9). Peter, Paul and Barnabas made statements about doctrine at a conference in Jerusalem, but James (not Peter) chaired the conference and delivered the final decision (Acts 15). Paul even corrected Peter at Antioch (Galatians 2:11-14).

Common sense should tell us that God would not build His Church on a mortal man, such as Peter or any other apostle; because they are tainted with sin (see for example Paul's telling comments in Romans 7:12-25) and have not yet been judged. Even believers, even those who are Christians are judged. Their judgment occurs at or immediately before the Judgment Seat of Christ (2 Corinthians 5:10). Those who did not know Jesus as their saviour during their life will be judged at the Great White Throne Judgment referred to in Revelation 20.

Long after the crucifixion, Peter himself wrote that he was merely a fellow elder: 1 Peter 5:1.

Furthermore, the following exchange took place when the Risen Jesus re-appeared to the eleven disciples in Galilee:

"Now the eleven disciples went into Galilee, to the mountain which Jesus had appointed for them to meet Him. And when they saw Him, they worshipped him; but some doubted. And Jesus came and spoke to them saying, 'All authority in heaven and on earth has been given to Me. Therefore, go and make disciples in all nations, baptising them in the name of the Father, and of the Son and of the Holy Spirit; teaching them to observe all things that I have commanded you'" Matthew 28:16-20).

Significantly, in this crucial exchange between the Risen Christ (who was also God the Son) and His mortal servants He told them that all authority had been given to *Him*, (not to *them*, or to one of them, such as Peter) to go into the world to make disciples in all nations teaching them to observe all the things that *Jesus* had commanded them to observe.

Plainly, Peter was not infallible. Jesus Himself prophesied, correctly that Peter would deny Him three times; as Peter duly did (Matthew 26:34; John 18:13-27). Nonetheless, the infallibility of the Pope in matters of faith and morals was proclaimed by the Vatican Council (that is, by men's egos) in 1970.

The correct position is that Jesus Christ is the one and only rock (1 Corinthians 10:4; 1 Peter 2:4; Isaiah 28:16); and He is the one and only gate or door to salvation – not the Pope, nor anyone else. The Pope is not your shepherd on Earth. If you appoint him as such you deny the sacrifice of Jesus, your one and only gateway.

The distortion by the RCC: It is fundamental to the entire structure of the RCC that Peter was the first 'Pope'. The Roman Catholic structure stands or falls on this tradition. Plainly, if Peter was not the first Pope and if he was not endowed with infallibility then the RCC's claim to divine authority through their line of Popes is baseless.

The doctrine of *Sola Scriptura* says that the opinions, beliefs and traditions of those who cannot point to a scriptural source are false. This would mean that the RCC bases for asserting that the Apostle Peter had a special standing among the Apostles and that his special standing has somehow been inherited by the Popes of Rome must be based on original Christian scripture to be true.

The concept of *Sola Scriptura* is supported by 2 Timothy 3:16, 2 Corinthians 2:13 and Romans 3:2.

It's clear from 1 Timothy 2:5 that only Jesus Christ can mediate between man and God; no one else; not Popes, not Saints, not Archbishops. Hebrews 4:14 makes clear that Jesus Christ is our one and only High Priest.

So why does the RCC claim that Peter was the first Pope and that members of the RCC somehow inherited his role? The answer is that they point to the words of Matthew 16:13-20 where Peter confesses Jesus as the Christ or Messiah, as being Divine. The point is that the deity of Christ comes only by divine revelation based on faith and Peter had shown faith in recognising who Jesus was.

The key to understanding this is verse 17:

"And Jesus answered and said to him 'Blessed are you Simon Bar-Jona, [Peter's full name was Simon Peter Bar-Jona] for flesh and blood [to flesh and blood you could add ego intellect] did not reveal it to you, but My Father, Who is in Heaven'."

Peter was just a fellow Elder. He himself said so (1 Peter 5:1). Jesus even rebuked Peter (Matthew 16:23). Furthermore, it seems that Peter went to Babylon, never to Rome, to preach (1 Peter 5:13). We know that the apostle Paul *was* in Rome and in his writings, he refers to Christians in Rome, but he never once names Peter as being there.

Paul was imprisoned twice in Rome, and was executed there during his second imprisonment. However, there's no mention of Peter ever being arrested or imprisoned in Rome. Paul wrote the Book of Romans in about 58 AD. There's no mention of Peter writing anything in Rome.

Peter, himself, declared that it was Jesus who was the Head and cornerstone of the Church (Acts 4:5-12). Refer also to John 6:44, Acts 2:38, Matthew 28:19.

In Colossians 1:18 the Apostle Paul confirmed that it was Jesus who is the Head of the Church. He said he same in 1 Corinthians 10:1-4, referring to Jesus as the Rock even in the time of Moses.

Second Distortion: The Mary Myth Created by the RCC...

What the Scripture actually says: The scriptures make clear that Mary should not be venerated, nor be the subject of prayers: Matthew 15:6, 8-9: Acts 1:14. The only scriptural reference that even remotely suggests that Mary might be worthy of worship is found in Luke 1:26-30. Mary was told by Gabriel that she is highly favoured and in Verse 30 that she has found favour with God. That hardly suggests that God has said that she will be or should be venerated, that she was sinless or had already been judged and found pure or righteous.

The distortion by the RCC: The exaltation of Mary formally commenced in the RCC in 431 CE when the term 'Mother of God' was applied at the Council of Ephesus. Prayers to Mary and dead 'Saints' became formalised in the RCC in 600 CE.

In 1854, the concept of the immaculate conception of Mary became part of RCC dogma. In 1950, the RCC adopted the doctrine of the assumption (bodily ascension) of the Virgin Mary into Heaven, shortly after her death. In 1965, Mary was proclaimed the Mother of the RCC.

Third Distortion: The Sabbath

What the Scripture actually says: The true Sabbath is Saturday, not Sunday. Sabbath-breaking and idolatry were the major reasons why God severely punished the ancient Israelites and drove them into slavery (Ezekiel 20; Matthew 22:2-3; Mark 10:11; Luke 5:14; Mark 2:27; Isaiah 56:6-7).

Distortion by the RCC: The RCC changed the Sabbath from Saturday to Sunday. This originated from the Roman Emperor Constantine who formalised Christianity as the Roman State religion but treated it more as a political tool.

Constantine convened the Council of Nicea in 325 CE. That council changed the Sabbath day from Saturday to Sunday as a political move to appease the Roman pagans and make the new State religion more convenient for them; because Sunday was the pagan day of worship of the Sun.

Fourth Distortion: Baptism

What the Scripture actually says: Baptism is an *essential* step in joining God's family. Baptism requires full immersion under water, not merely a sprinkling with droplets of water. (John 3:1-5; Colossians 2:12; Mark 16:15-16; Acts 2:38-41; Roman 6:3-4; Acts 2:38 and Matthew 28:19).

Furthermore, baptism is meant to follow repentance which means one must have an understanding of what one is doing at the time one is baptised. Therefore, infant baptism cannot have been intended.

Distortion by the RCC: The RCC accepts baptism other than by full immersion and accepts the baptism of infants.

Fifth Distortion: The RCC's Invention of the Concept of Purgatory...

What the Scripture actually says: According to the scripture, there is no such concept as 'purgatory'.

Distortion by RCC: A unique and mystifying doctrine of the RCC is 'purgatory', a place of burning torment that occurs between physical death and heaven.

The RCC teaches that one should pray for the dead who are in purgatory to hasten their purification and enable them to go to heaven that much sooner. The entire concept of purgatory is based on invented, false 'tradition' of the RCC rather than any scripture.

Sixth Distortion: Sacraments

What the Scripture actually says: The only 'sacrament' spoken of in the scriptures is Baptism following repentance.

Invention of Sacraments by the RCC...

The RCC has seven sacraments:

Baptism

Confirmation

Penance

Holy Eucharist

Marriage

Anointing the Sick

Holy Orders

Invention of Sacraments by the Protestants

The Protestants have two sacraments:

Baptism

Communion

Seventh distortion: Eucharist

What the Scripture actually says: There is no scriptural support for this practice.

Distortion by the RCC: The RCC points to John 6:51-55 as support for this concept; but Jesus made it clear in John 6:63 and Matthew 4:4 that he was speaking in relation to the spirit not the flesh.

According to the RCC, forgiveness of sins for the living and dead comes through this Eucharist and this sacrifice (that is, the Mass). This appears to be squarely at odds with Romans 8:1; Hebrews 9:14 and Hebrews 10:14.

Eighth Distortion: Idolatry

What the Scripture actually says: There is no support for idolatry in the scripture. On the contrary, the scripture teaches against idolatry, as is clear from the First Commandment (Isaiah 44:17; 45:20).

Distortion by the RCC: The RCC venerates Saints. The RCC pays homage to imagines (idols). Many Catholics pray to 'Saints' (that is, dead people). The RCC Catechism says at p645 #2683 that Catholics should ask Saints to intercede for them. They worship and pray to so-called holy relics.

Ninth Distortion: Mantras, Chanting, Repetition

What the Scripture actually says: Matthew 6:7 expressly prohibits mantras, chanting and repetitive 'prayers' as practised by '…the heathen…'

Distortion by the RCC: In direct contravention of the Bible's teaching the RCC practices 'Praying the Rosary', reciting a series of prayers that follow a predetermined sequence and terminology. The Rosary comprises a string with about 50 beads arranged in groups of ten called 'Decades'. Catholics are required to utter (chant) 20 decades in order to complete the Rosary.

To compound this breach of Bible teaching, one of the most common Rosary chants commences with the words 'Hail Mary'. She is often described as the 'Mother of God'.

Secular Religion… The Hoodlum Gang Ego… Political Correctness and Being 'Right'…

Ego driven social group narcissism is an all-pervading force in the west of the twenty-first century. We see examples of it every day, where indignant groups portray themselves as victims or saviours to bully those who don't agree with them into submission.

Common examples of the poison of political correctness are:

- accusations of racism at every conceivable opportunity
- denunciation of the long-held beliefs and values of Christian church groups
- maligning those who have worked hard and have, not surprisingly, ended up with more than their less hard-working neighbours

This general trend is sometimes described as political correctness but it's no more than disguised power mongering for self-gain or self-aggrandisement; and it's polarising societies by tearing down normal forms of discourse and preventing balanced, constructive debate. It's a social sickness.

A classic example can be found in the representatives of the Democratic Party of the US in the post Obama years; shocked and stunned, as they apparently were at their loss of the 2016 presidential election. Their often-hysterical attacks on their opponent's beggar belief and their motives seem to be transparent ego-driven self-interest. Their behaviour has set destructive new standards of what can be called belligerent 'progressive liberalism', where the distortion of facts, the use of half-truths and the disregard for long-standing social mores are undermining society.

This breed of politician, with their inflated narcissistic egos, typically depict any who disagree with them as liars, cheats, racists and law breakers. They portray their opponents as predators and those whose votes they seek to win as victims. They've brought us into an era that smacks of moral blackmail and political extortion.

These are serious issues because they are the vanguard of political agendas and political policies that undermine the long-held, legitimate moral values of a society, destroy its fabric, sow the seeds of division; and even undermine the nation's territorial sovereignty; the very things that elected representatives should be protecting and defending.

The anti-Brexit campaign is another example of an ego gang (the anti-Brexiteers) seeking to obstruct the implementation of the democratic vote of a majority of those Britons who bothered to vote in the 2016 Referendum to leave the EU.

Ego Snake Oil... Utopia For all the 'Victims'...

Many so-called wise men, self-appointed sages, have, through their intellectual egos, distracted and misled many others with their ideal world views. We've seen the reality of some of these models, such as fascism and communism, in recent history.

Fascism and communism are creations of the intellectual ego and each of them is flawed, because they're based on force, not on empowerment; not on truth or conscience.

The term 'utopia' was coined by Sir Thomas More (1478-1535) an English lawyer, social philosopher, author, politician and humanist. He is considered a leading scholar of his day. More wrote a good deal of historical stuff but he is probably best remembered for his book *Utopia*, written in Latin and published in 1516. It was translated into English in 1551, some years after his death. He was a committed Catholic, vehemently opposed to the Protestant Reformation. He proved a headache for the English King Henry VIII, was convicted of treason and executed. Henry VIII was, of course, at loggerheads with the Papacy so it's hardly surprising that the Catholic Church viewed Thomas More as a hero.

Pope Pius XI canonised More as a martyr in 1935. In 2000, Pope John Paul II declared him the Patron Saint of 'Statesmen and Politicians'. The Soviet Union also honoured More for his purportedly communistic attitude towards property.

The reason why utopia, communism, fascism, and even democracy, don't work is because they do not of themselves remove the ego from the social model. No model run by the ego can ever be successful, because it's force based.

If we accept what David Hawkins says then the only way that ego can be toppled from power is with an LoC of 500 or more on the Hawkins' MoC, because it's only at the level of 500 plus that the ego begins to lose its grip. Hawkins says that at LoC 500 love becomes a key driver; and, according to Hawkins, at LoC 540 love becomes Love (that is, unconditional). Hawkins is partly correct.

Jesus taught: unconditional love, first of God and secondly of your neighbour (Matthew 22:36-40). So, love is centred on God; and it comes from the humble heart, not from 'enlightenment' or a high LoC on Hawkins' MoC.

An Atheist Evolutionist's Ego View... The 'Elite' Come First...

In his extraordinary tirade, *The God Delusion* (2006), Oxford Biologist, Richard Dawkins lets his ego run riot. He passes judgment on God, and sentences Him to death. Dawkins preaches that God is a myth.

There's no doubt that Dawkins, and those who subscribe to his views, will, indeed, find out whether they are correct. If, as I would say, they're not correct then they've got problems because God has expressly warned humankind not to mock Him, His messengers, His prophets or His word; at the peril of facing His full wrath (2 Chronicles 36:16).

The Christian scripture is sprinkled with such warnings. For example, Matthew 12:31-32 warns:

"But whoever speaks against the Holy Spirit will not be forgiven in this age or in the age to come."

Christ warned that all humans will be held accountable for every idle word spoken (Matthew 12:36-37).

Nonetheless, Dawkins says (p36, *The God Delusion*) that he is:

"... attacking God, all gods, anything and everything supernatural, whatever and whenever they have been or will be invented."

It seems that the premise for Dawkins' leap to the conclusion that there cannot be a creator God is that the *theory* (it's a *theory* not a proven *law*) of spontaneous, non-divine human origin and biological evolution disproves God's existence because it disproves that God created man.

As an aside, we need to realise that many of the greatest scientists in history (far more noteworthy men than Richard Dawkins) were or are believers in God; such as Sir Isaac Newton and Johannes Kepler.

Nonetheless, the intellectual ego-driven message from Dawkins' book is that atheists are brave, noble and erudite; whereas believers in God are simple-minded, superstitious and just plain delusional (that is, insane).

Dawkins isn't the first to put forward these sorts of intellectual ego-driven pronouncements. Bertrand Russell had a shot at it back in 1927 with his essay, 'Why I am not a Christian'.

The Ego's Delusion of *Homo Deus*... The 'Elite' Come First... Again...

In *Homo Deus (A Brief History of Tomorrow)* (2016), Yuval Noah Harari, who has a PhD. in History from the University of Oxford, gives us his insouciant portend of what can only be described as a chilling future for humankind. Harari, himself, does not appear to see what he describes as horrific, which is all the more alarming; and all the more insightful when we consider the dangers posed by the intellectual ego.

When one has read *Homo Deus* what is revealed is a golem dystopia; a glimpse into a future that envisages the planned extermination of humans, and their replacement; initially with cyborgs and then with golem. This is an apocalyptic anti-human vision, and yet thousands are apparently in awe of Harari's writing.

Insight: The Latin words *Homo Deus*, literally mean 'man god' or 'god man'. This tells us that what Harari is proposing is that cyborgs or golems based on humans will become 'gods'.

Insight: A cyborg, or cybernetic organism, is a being with both organic and biomechatronic body parts. A cyborg is similar to an android, which can be entirely artificial or part biological. When it's part biological it's a cyborg. In effect, an android (from the Greek *androeides* meaning 'man-like') is a robot that resembles a human being. A cyborg may or may not resemble a human being. All androids are robots.

Insight: A 'golem' is an animate, soul-less anthropomorphic being created from inanimate matter.

Harari's book should serve as a warning to all of us to examine our minds and our hearts and ask: does our life have a purpose and meaning and if so, what is that purpose and what is that meaning? For his part, in *Homo Deus*, Harari offers absolutely no purpose and no meaning for human life; and he plainly gives it no value. In that regard he is in the same boat as atheists such as Richard Dawkins.

Harari's book is full of half-truths and untruths about the Christian scripture (for example, refer to page 55 of his book). Contrary to what Harari would have you believe the Christian scripture talks of a clear and definite purpose and a clear and definite future for humankind – and the choices that will determine our individual futures is in the hands of each of us. To me, we're presented with Harari's atheistic predictions verses Christian scriptural prophecy.

Insight: Whereas predictions are no more than speculation, Christian scriptural prophecy is history told in advance. There's a world of difference between the two.

In summary, Harari's predictions and his preferences are sinister. For example:

- He subordinates truth below order and power (p231)
- He believes ours is no more than a 'dog eat dog existence', and that 'might is right' (pp54, 238, 261)
- He yearns for science to engineer (that is, to replicate) human minds and when that happens, he foresees (and I believe he desires) that homo sapiens will 'disappear' (p53), because the cyborgs and golem will exterminate them
- He sees these golem as having "divine powers of creation and destruction" (p53) – not just powers but *divine* powers
- He says that these amortal beings (p29) "… could love, hate, create and destroy on a much grander scale than us" (p54)
- He declares that humans do not have souls (pp119 and 135)
- He says the theory of evolution (that is the theory of the spontaneous, non-divine origin and biological evolution of humans) cannot accept the idea of human souls because a soul has no parts, so it cannot possibly result from a step-by-step spontaneous, non-divine biological evolution (p122)

There's no question that Yuval Harari like Richard Dawkins is a God hater; he says God is myth (p134), he says God and the human soul belong in the dustbin of science (p134), and he says scientists today can do much better than God (p55).

One has to ask: what is Harari's agenda and what are his motives for such a rant against God and humanity? The answer is obvious. Like Richard Dawkins, Harari is a vehemently God-hating atheistic evolutionist anthropocentric.

Why is it that Harari (his ego) is so plainly desperate to have us (not just him but *us*) hate God, to deny the existence of God and to welcome the destruction of humankind? Is it ego? I'll leave that for you to ponder.

One also has to ask: who are people like Harari and Dawkins the agents of? I will also leave that for you to ponder. It's a question you *should* ponder, as it may affect you more deeply and more imminently that you realise.

The upshot of Harari's *Homo Deus* is:

- First, amortality is inevitable – which to this author's level of consciousness is atheistic nonsense
- Secondly, the Christian God is a myth (pp24-26, 29, 134) – and I am glad it is not me saying that
- Thirdly, we should only be interested in finding the key to 'happiness' (pp34, 40) – and one wonders if his ego means his happiness (and the happiness of his cronies) or your happiness?
- Fourthly, our goal should be to become cyborgs and golem and to acquire divine powers (pp53-54) – so we can love, hate, create and destroy on a much grander scale than we presently are capable of

The books by Richard Dawkins and Yuval Harari are eye-popping insights into the minds of so-called 'intelligent' humans, educated by other co-called intelligentsia, who plainly have very limited consciousness. It's apparent, in my view, that their egos are downright dangerous to your quest for higher consciousness.

What You Learned in This Chapter...

- The greatest prize in life is to become the best version of you that it's possible to be
- Your greatest tool in becoming the best possible version of you is humility, because the humble mind and heart are ripe for learning
- Your enemy to becoming the best version of you is your ego (and the egos of others) in all its manifestations
- Your ProtoEgo, the intellectual ego and the spiritual ego all suffer from vanity, pride, arrogance, fear, hubris and self-pity – so why would you allow them to guide you?
- To become the best version of you requires overcoming your ego and not being brought down by the egos of others
- You need to be extremely careful with the ancient sages (such a Buddha) and the New-Age sages (such as David Hawkins)

Chapter 9

The Unfolding Spiritual 'Consciousness'...

What You'll Discover in This Chapter...

- Human life isn't a random biological aberration – your life has a purpose
- There's been a spiritual awareness unfolding for man for about 5980 years, when Adam and Eve were in Eden, give or take about 11 years
- Unlike intellectual ability, spiritual awareness isn't of the mind, but of the heart and spirit
- There's nothing wrong with intellectual learning, per se, but its importance, its relevance, its standing, has to be kept in perspective or you risk ending up at a dead end – like Bertrand Russell (*Why I Am Not a Christian*), Francis Crick, Richard Dawkins (*The God Delusion*), Raymond Kurzweil, Stephen Hawking and Yuval Harari (*Homo Deus*)

What You Choose to be You Will Be... In the End...

The point of this book isn't to get you to become a Christian, or to get you to believe in God; or to stop being a Roman Catholic, a Buddhist or scientologist. You'll make your choices in life and I'll make mine and we'll both live with the consequences.

I'm not trying to convert anyone to anything; primarily because I know that's not my role. For Christians, it's not even for us to know whether or not our spouse should be called or converted. It's a matter for God (1 Corinthians 7:16).

Our task as Christians is to change ourselves not to try to convert or change others (Matthew 7:5).

Jesus said, "No one can come to Me unless the Father, who sent Me, draws him, and I will raise him up in the last day." (John 6:44; Matthew 13:10)

I merely wish to give you information that might help you find your way; because God has said that whoever brings one sinner to Him will have a multitude of sins covered (James 5:19-20). Faith without works is dead faith (James 2:17-24).

Insight: God is extraordinarily generous with the unbelieving members of a believer's family. These unbelievers may still be given blessings and protection (Acts 16:31; 1 Corinthians 7;12-14).

The big game...

The greatest challenge and opportunity in life is to find out whether your life has a purpose, and if so, what that purpose is; otherwise, you're on a pointless mortal journey, like Richard Dawkins and Yuval Harari.

In this book, I'm endeavouring to clear the path for you to make better enquiry, a full enquiry, and to come to better decisions, for you and your loved ones, by identifying and dealing with one of the greatest obstacle to truth, namely your ego; and that's it. In the end, you will be what you choose to be. If you choose to be your ego's version of you then so be it.

It's All About the Questions...

The most difficult part about solving a problem or a conundrum, such as the meaning of life, is figuring out what the question is, and how it is to be asked. That's where the wisdom, the insight, is. Once you've worked out the question it's only a matter of time before the answer appears, unless you give up looking. If you refuse to ask the questions you'll get an ego-driven outcome by default.

Insight: David Hawkins appears not to have asked the right questions when coming up with his MoC, which is why he concluded that the purpose of human life is 'obscure' (*Power vs Force*, p314).

Truth... And Ego Censorship...

The only questions that are really valuable are those that aren't censored by your ego; which means they cannot be questions from your intellect. The questions have to be honest, open questions to be of any use; which means that they must come from your heart. Questions based on invalid assumptions, half-truths or lies cannot lead to truth. Your ego has biases and an agenda so don't let it craft the questions. Your ego always wants to prove that its biases are 'right', so don't trust it to be impartial and honest. Be prepared to have your ego's preconceptions proved wrong.

The Unfolding Spiritual Consciousness... Bystanders and Participants...

Like it or not, those who don't find the true meaning and purpose of their lives are redundant, expendable. They may be filling in their time doing lots of 'important stuff' but their mortal life is being squandered.

Back To 3960 BC... Adam and Eve's Roller Coaster... You've Got a Ticket to Ride...

If we go back in time to the period after 'the Fall' when Adam and Eve were cast out of Eden there was an immediate overall steep decline in the faith index, the humility index and the happiness index for mankind, in general. In the first generation after the Fall Cain 'murdered' his brother Abel. We're talking about 5980 years ago (as at 2020), approximately 3960 BC.

Insight: The commonly held belief that the fifth commandment says you shall not 'kill' is wrong. The correct translation of Exodus 20:13 is that you shall not commit 'murder', which is an intentional killing that is not just *in the eyes of God*.

Let's Look at Our Spiritual Timeline...

Year	Description
3960 BC	Adam and Eve let their egos run wild and decide they know better than God. They learn of lawlessness from their (our) mortal enemy (Satan) whose agenda is to destroy them and their seed (us). Satan sells their ego his first big lie to humankind: that they are 'immortal' and will not, as God says, surely die, if they go on the wild side. Note: To this day man's ego is still pursuing immortality through science, but these efforts will fail.
3960 BC?	Once Adam and Eve leave Eden, they start having children. Cain (who later gets killed by Tubal Cain by being shot with an arrow) murders his brother Abel, out of jealousy of Abel and anger with God. Note: we know how Cain died from the Ancient Book of Jasher, referred to in 2 Timothy 3:8.

2304 BC	The Great Flood descends on the whole Earth because God is fed up with humankind, who indulge themselves in hedonistic pursuits, prey on their fellows, and worship false Gods created by their egos. The flood lasts just over a year. Only 8 people survive the flood (1 Peter 3:18-22).
2100 BC?	Nimrod, the great grandson of Noah, builds Babylon, in Mesopotamia. Note: 'Mesopotamia' means 'the land between 2 rivers' (referring to the Tigris and the Euphrates rivers, in what, today, is part of Iraq).
1850 BC?	Abram (later renamed Abraham) leaves Ur to go to the land of Canaan
2000 BC?	Abraham is sent by God to sacrifice Isaac at Mt Moriah
1487 BC – 1447 BC	Moses takes the Israelites out of the land of Egypt, across the Red Sea
1070 BC	David ordained as the King of the Israelites Note: This is the David, who, as a boy, slew Goliath (the Philistine)
1012 BC	King David dies (aged 70: 2 Samuel 5:4) and his son Solomon takes the throne
1007 BC	The construction of Solomon's Temple begins
972 BC	The kingdom of the Israelites is wracked by civil war and divides into the northern Kingdom of Israel and the southern Kingdom of Judah
740 BC to 720 BC	Assyria disperses the northern Kingdom of Israel and sends most of those Israelites, who became known as the 'Ten Lost Tribes', into exile (a diaspora)
590 BC	Babylon invades the Kingdom of Judah and sends most of its upper class to captivity in Babylon. Note: Approximately 70 years later the descendants of many of these captives (who had by now inter-married with Babylonians) are freed by Cyrus, King of the Medo-Persians, who conquered Babylon. They were allowed to return to Jerusalem but their religion had now been contaminated by pagan Babylonian beliefs. The descendants of these people become the Pharisees, Scribes and Sadducees of the time of Jesus
5 BC	Jesus is born between about 27 August and 9 September
30 AD	Wednesday, 5 April, between about 9:00 am and midday Jesus crucified at Passover (Nisan 14 of the Jewish calendar) dying at approximately 3:00 pm

The First Covenant... Adam Gets a Garden...

Adam and Eve were promised a bounteous life as the caretakers of God's Earth. Their blessings were guaranteed if they lived in righteousness, by obeying God. However, if they transgressed, they would lose this status. They were commanded not to eat from the tree of knowledge of good and evil. In other words, God had a covenant with Adam and Eve; and they broke that covenant; and now we don't live in an Eden.

The Second Covenant... Noah Goes Boating...

After the Great Flood, God covenanted with Noah that He would never again destroy the world by flood (Genesis 9) for Noah living righteously. Noah lived at a time when the whole Earth was filled with corruption and violence, but he didn't succumb to that behaviour. He stood out as the only one who "walked with God" (Genesis 6:9). This had also been true of Noah's great-grandfather Enoch (Genesis 5:22). Therefore, the Lord chose Noah to survive with his family when the Great Flood was unleashed.

The story of Noah is remembered in the New Testament (Hebrews 11:7). Noah became the heir of righteousness because of his faith. In other words, if we have the requisite faith, we will be treated by God as being righteous and will be accorded protection and salvation, and the rewards that follow, just as Noah was.

The Third Covenant... Abram (Later Re-Named Abraham) Heads West...

After Noah, the world again succumbed to sin. Nimrod, the great grandson of Noah, had such ego that he built the Tower in Babylon to show how great he was.

God therefore decided to call Abram (later re-named Abraham). He promised Abraham the land of Canaan, and a son and heir (Isaac). He promised blessings to Abraham's descendants.

Abraham was like a new Adam, and Canaan was like a new Eden; where God could dwell (in the hearts of) his people. So long as the children of Abraham had faith in the Lord and were righteous then the promised blessings would continue.

Insight: Only those of the faith are sons of Abraham (Galatians 3:6-9, 26, 29)

The Fourth Covenant... Moses and the Israelites Head East...

God established the Mosaic covenant after the freeing of Abraham's descendants from oppression in the foreign land of Egypt as prophesied in Genesis 15:12-15, and recorded by Moses in Exodus 19:4-6; 20:2. The covenant at Mt Sinai concerned how the Israelites, God's people, must conduct themselves within the land as an example nation (Exodus 19:5-6). They were to be God's 'treasured possession'. They were to be a 'holy nation' (Exodus 19:5-6).

The Mosaic covenant required Israel to adhere to the commandment in Exodus 20:23 that forbade them from making any gods of silver or gold. In today's parlance, we would talk about false gods such as Buddhism, environmentalism, humanism, and the like. They would be the equivalent of the golden calf made by the Israelites, because they amount to the worship of something other than God; such as the environment, 'mother earth', the sanctity of humanity (that is, putting humans on a pedestal), or worshipping so-called enlightened ones, such as Buddha.

The Davidic Covenant... The Building of a 'House' (That Is, a Dynasty)...

This covenant springs from the Prophet Nathan's message to David (2 Samuel 7; 1 Chronicles 17). David intended to build a temple for God but God promised to build a 'house' (that is, a dynasty) for David. This is referred to as a covenant in 2 Samuel 23:5; 2 Chronicles 7:18; 13:5; Psalms 89:3 and Jeremiah 33:21.

The Davidic covenant seems to follow on from the covenants with Abraham and Moses. God's plans for David and Israel are clearly intertwined with the previous covenants. There are significant parallels linking David to Abraham such as:

- God promising both a great name (Genesis 12:2; 2 Samuel 7:9)
- In the future, both would conquer their enemies (Genesis 22:17; 2 Samuel 7:11 and Psalm 89:23)
- Both would have a special standing (Genesis 17:7-8; 2 Samuel 7:24; Psalm 89:26)
- There would be a special line of 'offspring' perpetuating both their names (Genesis 21:12; 2 Samuel 7:12-16)
- The descendants of both were required to keep God's laws (Genesis 18:19; 2 Samuel 7:14; Psalm 89:30-32 and 132:12)
- The offspring of both would mediate international blessing (Genesis 22:18 and Psalm 72:17)

The Davidic covenant therefore identifies more precisely the lineage of the 'offspring' who will mediate international blessing.

The New Covenant of Jesus...

All the previous covenants failed – and I would put that down to human ego taking precedence over faith in God and humility; with the resulting disasters that beset humankind.

In the case of the Israelites, they warred with each other resulting in them splitting into two kingdoms: the Kingdom of Judah (primarily the tribes of Judah, Levi and Benjamin) and the Kingdom of Israel (being the other tribes, albeit with a few from the tribes of Judah, Levi and Benjamin). In turn, these kingdoms were conquered and vanished.

This could have been the end of God's plans but of course He had a back-up, because He knew full well what the human ego is like.

Therefore, God took the final step of sending Jesus (God the Son, part of the Elohim) to Earth to be the ultimate sacrifice and to provide the gateway to salvation for us on an *individual* basis, rather than on a *national* (that is, Israelite) basis.

Insight: The making of the New Covenant was prophesied in Jeremiah 31:31. In the Book of Isaiah, this everlasting covenant of peace is referred to several times (Isaiah 42:6; 49:8; 54:10; 55:3 and 61:8).

This New Covenant was different in that it was not limited to the Israelites.

So, What do the Covenants Mean...?

In short, none of us is denied the opportunity to have faith in God, to practise humility, to read the scriptures and to try to fulfil our mortal earthly purpose by being found to be righteous; in which case, we will be given God's grace and God can shower us with the rewards that He wishes to bestow on us.

Paul's Message of Encouragement (Romans 7)...

In January 2009, the author watched a DVD sermon by Rod King of the Living Church of God ('LCG') entitled *The Third Law*. This chapter is inspired by and very much based on the author's understanding of what Mr King had to say. The sermon was, in this author's view, perceptive, insightful, instructive and of enormous value to anyone seeking to fulfil the purpose for which he or she was created.

In the DVD sermon Mr King said that the 'first' law comprises the Commandments and Statutes crafted by our Creator as our code of conduct for our mortal lives. God tells us that His Commandments "… are not burdensome" (1 John 5:3). This is self-evident because obedience to His code doesn't result in us being denied anything, but actually enables us to qualify for abundance in our earthly life and to qualify for the rewards of eternal life.

For this reason, it is in our own interests, to our benefit, that we obey God's laws. We are being told that we will prosper by doing so. Jesus taught that adherence to God's laws would bring all manner of rewards to us (Matthew 19:16-21). He also taught that if you break one commandment you break them all (James 2:10).

Jesus made it clear that He came to fulfil the law not to destroy it and that God requires of each of us that we obey His laws if we wish to qualify for eternal life (Matthew 5:17-20). Obviously, if, as the scriptures say, the law is exulted by God (Isaiah 42:21) then the law is not dead, but is there for each of us to obey; because it is holy, just and good (Romans 7:12).

Most importantly, unless we develop a monotheistic rather than an anthropocentric (or humanist) mindset we cannot become subject to God's law (Romans 8:7) and cannot therefore please God (Romans 8:8) with the result that we cannot qualify for eternal life. This means that you cannot be both a humanist and a Christian – you're one or the other.

Mr King says in this DVD that the second 'law' is evidenced by the dilemma highlighted by the Apostle Paul in Romans 7:13-14. Paul said that he knew that the law is spiritual but he was carnal, sold under sin (v14).

Paul said that although he intended to and wanted to practice God's law he often, instead, disobeyed that law (v15).

Paul said that he was often guilty of acting contrary to the law notwithstanding that he agreed that the law is good (v16); and he put this down to the fact that it was not a disobedience that he chose to engage in but one that resulted from "… sin that is dwelling in me." (v17 and v20).

Paul then stated: "Consequently, I find this law in my members, that when I desire to do good, evil is present with me." (v21)

Paul was saying that although we hate sin and love God's law, we still knowingly sin; but as long as we strive, genuinely, to be obedient then we are saved by the blood of Jesus.

If, however, we merely pay lip-service to God's laws then the blood of Jesus cannot save us; because the blood of Jesus can only avail the righteous (those who do not make a *practice* of sinning).

Insight: Paul said we *knowingly* sin, but he did not say that we *practise* sinning. The difference is crucial.

This second law being referred to by Paul can probably be described as the law of ongoing choice that is imposed on us, daily, as part of our road-test by God to hone us into the very best we are capable of becoming and therefore qualifying us for the highest position and the greatest rewards we are capable of achieving in God's spiritual kingdom.

Mr King says that the third 'law' is evidenced by the spirit of life in Jesus Christ. He says that the third 'law' is to the effect that we cannot, of our own will or desire or effort, live a sinless, perfect life.

Mr King points out that it is for this reason (because we realise that we are incapable of living a perfect, sinless life) that some of us, including professing Christians, invented the fiction that God's laws (the Ten Commandments) were nailed to the cross with Jesus; because they wrongly believe that they have to be sinless; so they invented the lie that the law was nailed to the cross.

The true position is, as stated by Mr King, that the operation of the third law (that is, the ongoing effect of Jesus' sinless life and His sacrifice for our sin) frees us from the second law (that is, our inability to be sinless) so that we can keep the first law (that is, practice obeying the Commandments).

To put it another way, Mr King is, as I understand him, is reminding us that we are not required to be sinless for salvation but we must *practice* not sinning.

The point Mr King makes is profound and its understanding enhances our prospects for living righteously (which we can only do by not making a habit of sinning, by not *practicing* sin) by honestly and genuinely striving to obey God's laws and seeking forgiveness through prayer every time we fall short, thereby keeping open the lines of communication between us and God. If we do this, God will forgive us (1 John 1:7-9).

Insight: The position espoused by Mr King must be correct because Jesus gave His life to answer not only for the original sin (that is, the sin of Adam and Eve) but to provide a mechanism for the expunging of *these* sins, that is the sins that those who practice righteousness still succumb to.

Insight: By inventing the fiction of the laws being nailed to the cross many confused, misguided or disingenuous professing Christians are, in effect, worshipping a dead Jesus rather than a living Jesus. They ignore the fact that He lives and sits on the right hand of God and that He (Jesus) will judge the nations

(Matthew 25:31-34) and judge us as individuals (Matthew 7:21-23; John 5:21-22). Why would He need to judge us if the laws were nailed to the cross?

Insight: If the laws were nailed to the cross, then surely even Satan and the demons (and the likes of Hitler, Stalin and serial murderers) qualify for salvation, but we know that they will go to the Lake of Fire to answer for their sins.

Not only is Jesus alive and sitting on the right hand of God in Heaven, He is also alive on Earth living in those who have chosen to be righteous (obedient to God). Paul said: "I have been crucified with Christ, yet I live. Indeed, it is no longer I, but Christ lives in me. For the life that I am now living in the flesh, I live by faith – that very faith of the Son of God, Who loved me and gave Himself for me" (Galatians 2:20).

The life led by these apostolic Christians must be aimed towards selflessness, striving for the same heart (obedience to God's laws) as was personified in Jesus (Philippians 2:3-11).

As the Apostle John taught, by living in this way, apostolic Christians are not living so much as themselves (not anthropocentrically, not carnally) but as conduits for the will of God (John 5:30).

Insight: It is through obedience to God's law, through striving for righteousness, in God's eyes, through emulating Jesus Christ to the very best of our ability, that we open ourselves to the Holy Spirit which then dwells in us; and we allow the sacrifice of Jesus to work for us. It's a living, ongoing sacrifice, not a dead, finite sacrifice.

After the Fall of Adam and Eve man's ego took over to the point where God tried to sort us out with Noah, the ark and a lot of water; and later gave Moses the Ten Commandments whereby the ancient Israelites should live.

By that time, humankind in general was being driven by the ProtoEgo, supported by a spiritual ego that made gods in its image; and the Israelites built the statute of the golden calf. The ancient Israelites were meant to be an exception in that they were meant to be monotheistic; but they were more-or-less as morally bankrupt as their neighbours; which is what led to them losing their kingdoms of Israel and Judah in turn to the Assyrians and the Babylonians.

Insight: Today's Jews and Israelis are not the descendants of the Israelites, but that's another story.

According to Dr Hawkins' research, using the MoC (*Truth v Falsehood*, p37), the LoC for mankind generally was below LoC 90 until sometime after the birth of Buddha in about 563 BC. It then took until the birth of Jesus, over five centuries later, for the average to reach LoC 100. According to Hawkins, it only reached an average of LoC 100 because there were a handful of people whose LoCs exceeded 200 and they were dragging up the average; but the Earth was still a savage, lawless place, because it was running on the fuel of ego – as it still is.

It then apparently took nearly nineteen centuries for the average LoC to reach 205 (which it did in the late 1980s); and by the end of 2003 it had moved to LoC 203, then spiked briefly at LoC 207, before quickly dropping back to LoC 204. These calibrations vary according to the region of the world you're looking at; but everywhere you look there is ego-driven conflict and despair.

According to Hawkins (*Reality, Spirituality and Modern Man*, p35), approximately 85% of mankind still calibrated below the critical consciousness level of LoC 200 as at 2008. For the USA the percentage below LoC 200 was 55% as at 2008 after falling briefly to 49% in 2005.

According to Hawkins, this collective negativity of humankind is counterbalanced by the minority of people on the planet who are above LoC 200; but that's not an answer, a solution or anything to feel happy about, given the state the world is in; the state – spiritually and emotionally – that we're in. But how can Hawkins be correct given the dreadful state of the Earth and of man?

What You Learned in This Chapter...

- David Hawkins' MoC is far from complete and cannot be a spiritual guide
- The Christian scripture is the only reliable guide

Chapter 10
How You Know Your Ego's in Charge...

What You'll Discover in This Chapter...

- If negative events are recurring in any aspects of your life (such as relationships) a good place to look for the cause is your ego, someone else's ego or a combination of conspiring or warring egos
- Your ProtoEgo is in charge of your physical survival, in times of physical danger, and that's not necessarily a bad thing
- However, your ego also manifests in the intellectual and spiritual areas of your life and that can make you 'incompatible', and even hostile and belligerent

Your Ego Millstone...

Humans are extraordinary beings whenever they practice at the higher levels of being human; something every one of us is capable of doing. Yet, for much of their lives, most people are fearful, pessimistic, afraid to show love, they feel unloved; they are scared of life and afraid of death.

These negative feelings are safely kept in our ego box of fear, self-pity and victimhood. We think that others have it easier, or easy, compared to us, and that leads our ego to envy, covet, desire, and blame; and this extends to blaming God.

Your ego will use fear, self-pity and victimhood to keep you at the centre of things and it will always be able to find a scapegoat for all your worldly woes. What it won't do is undertake a journey of self-examination, a self-audit or self-awareness. It will only ever have ego awareness.

Even Atheists Blame God...!

Richard Dawkins is an avowed atheist, by anyone's measure. His vitriolic book, *The God Delusion*, an extraordinary atheistic rant, is all the proof you need for this.

Deep inside, I think Richard Dawkins (his ego) fears God, and he, therefore, feels the need to attack Him. Otherwise, he wouldn't have felt the need to write such a book; to try desperately to persuade you and me not to believe in God. He wrote it so his ego won't be alone, and won't be even more afraid of what lies ahead for him.

I say this after having read *The God Delusion* quite closely. So, now, I'm going to look at his book as a way of showing how empty and devoid of value our egos really are.

If we scrutinise *The God Delusion,* we find it's full of flaws. I deal with some of them in the following paragraphs.

Dawkins' book is in two parts. In the first part (up to p.159) Dawkins the scientist (the evolutionist) tries to convince us that evolution proves that God doesn't exist. In the second part of his book, Dawkins the (self-proclaimed) theologian gives us his analysis of the scriptures and his take on theology. Okay, now to his book.

We learn straight away that Dawkins is very sensitive to the giants of science such as Einstein being quoted as supporting belief in God. Dawkins coins the term 'Einsteinian religion' (p.19) in an attempt to persuade his readers that Einstein didn't really believe in God; not that it matters, except, apparently, to Dawkins.

But let's look at Einstein, anyway. Dawkins' first problem, and Einstein's first problem, is that they confuse 'religion' and 'scripture'. I have made the point that the Roman Catholic and Protestant churches have embellished or interpreted the scripture and thereby falsified it; that they have, by doing so, created 'religion'.

There is no evidence that I'm aware of that Einstein ever studied theology or studied the Christian scripture or claimed to have any knowledge of them. Therefore, his views and the views of all other such scientists, past and present, are irrelevant.

What scientists may think is of no account. God will judge *you*. When He does so, He will not be the slightest bit interested in the views of Einstein,

Dawkins or anyone else. He will be interested in *you*. It won't do you any good to answer a wrathful God by saying: "But Dawkins said…"

As much as he tried, Einstein, like many other eminent scientists, couldn't help but think that there must be a supreme being. Einstein is quoted by Dawkins (*The God Delusion*, p.19) as saying that he preferred not to call himself 'religious', because, as he apparently put it: to "… the vast majority of people, 'religion' implies 'supernatural.'"

According to Dawkins, Einstein conceded that he was 'religious' in the sense of being in awe of the things that science cannot grasp, but he added that those things may not be 'forever ungraspable'.

This 'awe' that Einstein referred to is the starting point for obtaining knowledge of God. Unfortunately, Albert appears not to have taken it further.

No doubt, if humankind survives long enough, many more things of the natural world will be discovered by man but those discoveries will not prove or disprove God's existence. God is only of the natural world to the extent that He created it, and created the things that are within it, and is a theist God. He is Spirit (John 4:24). Science will never build models or theories that will discern God because science cannot discern that which is of the Spirit.

Plainly, Dawkins' description (p.31) of God as a malevolent destroyer of things and people is idiotic. Firstly, why should God wish to destroy the things He has been at pains to create? Secondly, it isn't God, but humankind, that's guilty of the wrongs that Dawkins describes in his book.

It's true that God has punished humankind, severely, in the past and He will do so again. He has done this to rid the world of evil; evil that existed (and exists) only as a result of God's laws being broken. He's done this in the hope of bringing an end to lawless conduct. However, God has given each of us freedom of choice and freedom of conduct, because God is road-testing each of us to see if we're suitable material to join His Family. He can't road-test us if we have no free will; what would be the point?

On pages 34-35 Dawkins refers to persons canonised by the Roman Catholic Church who were involved in wrong-doing. Of course they were; they were human; and all humans have been involved in wrongful conduct; you, me and Richard Dawkins included.

Dawkins could have also added that one of the Popes (Alexander VI) was a Borgia (1431-1503); Pope from 1492 to 1503. His immorality is legendary and epic.

The point is, these humans were engaging in *their* conduct, *their* misconduct. It was not God's conduct. More to the point would be for Dawkins to ask: did Jesus ever conduct Himself in such a way? This is the relevant question to ask because Jesus came to provide us with a model and with the gateway for our salvation.

Dawkins asserts (p.37) that Christianity was founded by Paul of Tarsus. That's news to anyone with any scriptural knowledge. Christianity was founded by and on Jesus Christ. That's why it is called 'Christianity'. Jesus is the cornerstone of Christianity (Ephesians 2:19-22; Psalm 18:22-23; Isaiah 28:16; Matthew 21:42-44; 1 Corinthians 3:11; 1 Peter 2:6-8; Acts 4:11).

Dawkins says (p.37) that, for his purposes, Judaism, Christianity and Islam can be treated as indistinguishable. These three belief systems cannot be treated as indistinguishable for *any* purpose. For starters, the God of Judaism and Christianity is by no means the same being as the Allah of Islam.

Dawkins goes completely haywire at pages 49-54. Firstly, he concedes that he cannot disprove the existence of God (having nonetheless stated, unequivocally, that God does not exist) but suggests that the disproof of God can be found in "… the shading of probability." What on Earth is the *shading* of probability in the context of the non-natural world? This is another way of saying: Let's pretend we don't have to disprove God's existence to show that He doesn't exist.

Dawkins demonstrates the intellectual ego's well-developed talent for double standards (p.54) with this offering: "That you cannot prove God's non-existence is accepted and trivial, if only in the sense that we can never absolutely prove the non-existence of anything. What matters is not whether God is disprovable (he isn't) but whether his existence is 'probable'."

In the very next paragraph Dawkins says, in response to the argument that he cannot disprove God's existence, that that may be so but as an argument it is "… undeniable but ignominious and weak." Really? Ignominious? Weak? Sounds, strong and compelling to me.

Dawkins savagely attacks the scientist Alistair McGrath for gainsaying him. He scorns McGrath by referring to what Dawkins calls "… one of McGrath's less admired books, *Rocks of Ages.*" Dawkins criticises McGrath for having coined the acronym NOMA to describe what McGrath calls 'non-overlapping magisteria'.

One can sense a degree of ego petulance and ego rage by Dawkins when confronted with arguments he cannot overcome. On page 56, he complains to the effect that it is tiresome that he constantly hears: "That science concerns itself with *how* questions, but only theology is equipped to answer *why* questions." What on Earth Dawkins complains "is a why question?" You and I can easily see the difference, so why can't Dawkins?

This is a childish ego-driven cop-out by Dawkins, and a few sentences later he more or less admits it: "Perhaps, there are some genuinely profound and meaningful questions that are forever beyond the reach of science... But if science cannot answer some ultimate questions, what makes anybody think that religion can?" 'Religion' doesn't. The scriptures do.

Dawkins pronounces (pp.58-59): "The presence or absence of a creative super-intelligence is unequivocally a scientific question, even if it is not in practice – or not yet – a decided one." In an attempt to shore up this dubious point Dawkins then reels off a list of silly questions; ignoring the fact that there are contemporaneous eye-witness reports on the very questions he poses.

On page 73, Dawkins launches his next submission (totally unsupported in any way) which in his words "... goes to the heart of this book." Here it is:

"Entities that are complex enough to be intelligent are products of an evolutionary process."

That's Dawkins' argument; and, apparently, his evidence.

In other words, because Dawkins believes it, it must be so. This makes the title of my book so apt for the likes of Dawkins: *It must be true... I made it up myself...!*

Dawkins then has a shot at Thomas Aquinas (p.80). He calls Thomas' arguments or proofs of God's existence 'ontological' (that is, concerning the essence of abstract things). Dawkins describes Thomas' discourse as "... argument... which is the language of the playground." Ironically, Dawkins' entire book is ontological.

Dawkins accuses Thomas of stating (these are Dawkins' words, not Thomas'): "Bet you I can prove God exists." Thomas said nothing of the kind.

Yet, Dawkins' entire book is saying: "Bet you I can prove God doesn't exist."

Dawkins (pp.92-97) makes a number of unsupported attacks on the Bible.

For example, he asserts: "When the gospels were written, many years after Jesus' death, no one knew where he was born." The scriptures tell us where Jesus was born (Matthew 2:1-2; Luke 2:1-7). What's more the Old Testament prophet Micah prophesised the birthplace of Jesus in about 700 BC (Micah 5:2).

Next Dawkins asserts that the Apostle Luke has made mistakes in his writings. But Dawkins doesn't substantiate this; except to tell us that another atheist author (Wayne Fox) has 'concluded' this.

Dawkins then refers to alleged contradictions identified by Tom Flynn in the December 2004 issue of *Free Inquiry*. Flynn, like Dawkins, makes sweeping assertions such as: "Roman records mention no such census…" in response to scriptural and historical evidence (such as Luke 2) that there was such a census; at the instigation of the Syrian Governor: Quirinius. It is agreed however that modern historians say they can't find records of this census

You might ask, as I do: how can Flynn possibly make such an assertion!

Flynn asserts that Matthew and Luke give differing genealogies for Jesus: but he dismisses the simple explanation that one was the paternal line and the other was the maternal line.

Dawkins says (p.96): "The four gospels that make it into the official canon were chosen, more or less arbitrarily, out of a larger sample…" The selection wasn't arbitrary. The scriptures refer to false apostles who were shunned by true Christians (2 Corinthians 11:1-4; Jude 3-4; Revelation 2:2). It began with Simon Magus who syncretised (blended) old, pagan Babylonian beliefs with Christianity. Jesus Himself warned of this. He told a Samaritan woman that the Samaritans did not even know what they worshipped; that the truth that leads to salvation had been preserved by the Jews, not by the Samaritans (John 4:22).

Insight: Many books, even books cited by the apostles (such as the Book of Jasher, cited by Timothy: 2 Timothy 3:8) do not form part of the scripture because they are merely historical.

Dawkins asserts (p.96) that these missing gospels would have highlighted falsehoods in the scriptures or undermined the premise for belief. He's wrong yet again. The books of the New Testament were written during the lifetimes of the apostles; they are based on eyewitness accounts. The apostles themselves were eyewitnesses.

Dawkins criticises eminent scientists who believed in God (such as Sir Isaac Newton) (pp.97-103). What Dawkins appears to be saying is that if he could have had a good chat to these fellows, they would immediately have become atheists.

Having scorned the scientist-believers or claiming they probably only believed in God because of the social pressure of their times, he lauds the scientists who are atheists; inferring that their brave, atheistic stance bespeaks their inherent nobility and high principles. That's his ego at work.

In the case of Gregor Mendel (the Augustinian Monk who is one of Dawkins' heroes) Dawkins says that the only reason Gregor was a Monk was because it was the easiest way for him to pursue his science; but he hasn't referred to any writings of Gregor or any other evidence that suggests this.

Dawkins then gets really silly (pp.102-103) and tells us to the effect that there have been research studies that show that people with higher IQs tend to be atheists and the dummies tend to be believers.

What's God's Take on Dawkins and His Ego Ilk...?

God knows that scoffers like Dawkins will be trumpeting their views across the landscape as the end-times near. It's prophesied it in the Bible (Matthew 24:3-5; 11). God has given man a limited time to 'do it man's way' before He takes control and brings eternal peace to save us from ourselves, from rampant human ego in all its forms.

But God also gave a blunt warning to the self-proclaimed intellectual elite of this world:

"Woe to those who call evil good, and good evil... woe to those who are wise in their own eyes... because they have rejected the law of the Lord of Hosts, and despised the word of the Holy One of Israel. Therefore, the anger of the Lord is aroused..." (Isaiah 5:20-25).

God help Dawkins, before it's too late for him!

Back to Hawkins' MoC and Your Ego...

One of the drawbacks I see with Hawkins' MoC is that it doesn't directly address the ego, in any guise, and it cannot really do so because the MoC purports to be about stages of consciousness, or lack thereof; whereas the story of the ego is a parallel story; a story of domination of you and of others.

Nonetheless, in an indirect way the MoC identifies many of the attributes of the ego. Primarily, on the MoC, these attributes appear below the level of LoC 200, as you might expect. If you go to Chapter 18 and look at the extract I made of the MoC, then every attribute below LoC 200 describes your ego, and mine. It's not pleasant reading: and it's a constant struggle, at least for me, not to succumb to those attributes, but when I do succumb, I know my ego is running the show.

So, in a sense, the MoC could be said to show you the attributes you will exhibit (below LoC 200) when you're being ego-driven, and (above LoC, in stages) when you're pulling against your ego.

The Missing Ego Threshold on the MoC...

For the purposes of what I'm writing about there's a lot missing from the MoC; but the key missing attribute is humility. Nowhere on the MoC is there a reference to humility; and I'd say that's because it didn't register with Hawkins; it wasn't on his radar screen when he devised the MoC; it wasn't relevant.

To me, the absence of humility from the MoC tells me that Hawkins didn't, as I would put it, realise that his consciousness is not the supreme level of being or awareness; and it's not even a high level of being.

This is why he wrote so much about 'enlightenment' in this mortal life whilst acknowledging that he had no idea what the purpose or meaning of human life is; which is why he was of the view, mistakenly in my belief, that the meaning of life remains 'obscure' (*Power vs Force*, p314). This is probably also why he came to the bizarre view that only those below LoC 600 on his MoC require salvation (*The Eye of the I*, p404).

Insight: What this tells us is that you might, according to Hawkins' test, get a high score on his MoC and yet still be ignorant about who or what you are in the most fundamental of respects, by having no idea what the purpose or meaning of your life is. You might end up 'enlightened' – which can only mean not entirely ignorant – but you would never become informed, or righteous or aware of truth.

It's a serious issue that Hawkins couldn't fathom the meaning of life. This means the concept of righteousness could never register on his MoC.

This also helps explain why Hawkins got it so wrong with his assessment of the scripture; because he might have had a good level of 'consciousness', but faith (also missing from his MoC) is a matter of the heart not the intellect, not of 'consciousness'.

Insight: David Hawkins' MoC is a chart of the mind and intellect, which means it's of limited if any value when it comes to the spiritual.

Your ego might be your star-sign, horoscope, or tarot card reading... but inside you're a person...

I happen to know that I'm a Scorpio, I was born in the year of the Ox, and on the Myers Briggs type indicator (MBTI) I'm an INTJ. I don't put any stock in the first two but I do sometimes ponder the fact that I am (my ego is?) an INTJ while my wife of more than four decades is an ESFP. By the way, she's also a Virgo, and was born in the year of the Dragon.

My wife and I should not have survived our teenage dating let alone had a marriage of over 40 years, because we're supposedly incompatible. So what went wrong with the zodiacs and MBTI stuff? Why are my wife and I still together?

The answer is that we're only incompatible with others to the extent that we or they let ego run the show; to the extent that we subordinate our capacity for humility, conscience, forgiveness and engaging the wisdom of our heart, below our ego.

Insight: Incompatibility is an inevitable consequence of ego; which is essentially selfish, demanding and antagonistic; always portraying itself as 'wronged', as the victim, as 'deserving'.

What Is Humility...?

Is humility a sign of weakness, indifference, cowardliness? To your ego, especially your ProtoEgo, the answer is probably 'yes', because it always wants to be at the head of the queue; but that's a queue that's going nowhere.

Jesus gave us the greatest lesson in humility by divesting Himself of His divine status as part of the Elohim, to be born a mere mortal in order to provide us with a path to salvation; a path to His Kingdom. In His mortal form He was made a little lower than the angels (Hebrews 2:9).

No one else, not Buddha, Krishna not any mantra-chanting sage or contortionist yogi, has done anything, given anything, that can even begin to compare with what Jesus gave mankind; and He has even more in store: promised rewards, for those who truly accept His gift. What have Buddha and Krishna got in store for us? Why are they being extolled let alone worshipped?

Insight: The path to salvation (another concept not found on Hawkins' MoC) is something no one other that the Jesus has offered (John 1:29) or could ever offer (John 14:6; Romans 3:10; Galatians 3:10-11). It's a narrow path (Matthew 7:14) and can be trodden only by those who are righteous; and you cannot start to become righteous unless you first begin to practice humility. The path to salvation will not be found by vain, ego-driven, worldly men of hubris; and not will it be found through so-called 'enlightenment'.

Dust Should be Humble...

Man was created by God from the dust of the ground (Genesis 2:7) which was also created by God (Genesis 1:1). I think this was a deliberate decision by God; to remind us of our humble origins; to remind us that we are miraculous creations only because of the gifts He, alone, could give to dust.

Insight: Humility is the antidote for ego.

What You Learned in This Chapter...

- David Hawkins' MoC is incapable of leading you to truth given that he could not even figure out the meaning and purpose of his own life
- ego is a mortal disease and the antidote is humility, which is found in the heart not in 'consciousness'.

Chapter 11
Consciousness, Emotions, Feelings and Instincts...

What You'll Discover in This Chapter...

- Earthly, mortal man is not a complete being
- There's a difference between emotions, feelings and instincts, on the one hand, and consciousness, on the other, and the difference is the presence or absence of ego
- There are instincts that are ProtoEgo driven and there are instincts derived from consciousness, and they are different
- You determine how you 'feel' about something and how you feel determines who you are and what you can become

Stages of Consciousness...?

We've looked in some detail at David Hawkins' MoC with its various LoCs; including the two critical LoC levels: 200 and 500.

However, there are other ways of looking at consciousness, including the four stages of consciousness that was the subject of much work by Peter Ouspensky (1878-1947), an émigré to England from Czarist Russia.

Ouspensky was well-known in his time. He gave a series of lectures in New York in 1945, "The Psychology of Man's Possible Evolution", and it's probable that a young David Hawkins (1927-2012) knew of Ouspensky's work.

I don't perceive any of Ouspensky's work in the MoC. The approaches of Ouspensky and Hawkins appear to me to be different; but the work of Ouspensky is, nonetheless, interesting to me for the light it possibly, inadvertently, shines on the ego, as I have sought to explain it: the ProtoEgo, intellectual ego and religiou ego. Of course, neither Hawkins nor Ouspensky saw it this way, but I see an overlap of sorts nevertheless.

Ouspensky had some interesting views on what psychology really is, as opposed to how it's often described, and what it actually studies. He considered the label 'psychology' to be a new description for what in effect is a field of study that is ancient, that has been at the centre of various belief systems including Christianity. After all, take man out of Christianity and it loses its meaning and purpose.

To Ouspensky, psychology was most accurately described as the study of man's possible 'evolution', what I would call 'transformation'. He made clear in the first of his 1945 NYC lectures that he wasn't talking about man's biological evolution. He also made clear that in his view the Darwinian concept of the origin of man cannot be accepted; and in that regard he was on the same page as David Hawkins and me.

Man Is not a Complete Being…

Most insightfully, and perhaps harking back to the long-held views of the ancient world, including the world of Jesus, Ouspensky saw that man, in his current state, is not a complete being; that we are born with certain abilities and capabilities that each of us may develop to a greater or lesser degree; and with an inherent, non-intellectual, ability to develop further by our own efforts. If we fail to do so, we stagnate or even degenerate as human beings.

When you think about it, Ouspensky's views reflect to a degree what was subsequently refined by David Hawkins in his MoC. Both were talking of man developing consciousness rather than merely increasing his intellect and his knowledge of the earthly and the worldly and thereby stagnating, or worse.

The Obstacles to Man's Evolution of Consciousness…

As Ouspensky described it in his 1945 NYC lectures:

- For man to evolve his consciousness requires the development of inner qualities – and I would say requires man to develop the attitudes referred to in David Hawkins' MoC from LoC 200 upwards – which usually remain undeveloped or underdeveloped and cannot develop spontaneously of themselves

- This development of consciousness can occur only in special conditions – and I would add that those conditions are available to all and do not derive from or require intellectual capacity or prowess, which is an earthly, worldly attribute that can be an impediment to consciousness
- This evolution of consciousness will not happen automatically, it requires enormous personal effort and it requires help from another source – and I would add that the only source that can help is one of existing higher consciousness (that is an ego-less or ego-lesser source) and that those of only higher intellect are of no value in this exercise
- Not all of us will develop to a higher level of consciousness because some are not prepared to surrender their intellects (that is, their ego view points) – they are not prepared to surrender what they currently are which is an essential step in this transformation
- Evolving one's consciousness effectively makes man into an entirely different being even though he will remain in his earthly mortal state
- In effect man must acquire qualities that the foolish man – the man of ego intellect – already erroneously believes he possesses and the foolish man thereby fatally deceives himself, because he cannot see what he lacks
- Man deceives himself by believing he has powers and capacities which he ascribes to himself – that his ego ascribes to him – but which in reality he does not have
- Man lives the delusion of believing he is 'conscious' when in fact he is not – as I would put it, consciously thinking, on the one hand, and consciousness, on the other hand, are not the same

Ouspensky's Four States of Consciousness...

Ouspensky's view was that man has possibly four states of consciousness:

- Sleep state, which he says is a subjective, passive state, the lowest state of consciousness, with no real direction, no logic, no sequence
- Waking state, which he says is little different from the sleep state, but in which we talk, think, work and perceive of ourselves as conscious beings
- Self-consciousness state, being what man (that is, man's ego) ascribes to himself, what man thinks he possesses

- Objective consciousness state, of which man in his ordinary life experiences and knows nothing

Interestingly, Ouspensky was of the view that the Christian teachings, the Gospel, is one that says that man lives in a state of sleep and must first awaken for him to understand who and why he is.

Ouspensky espoused that we generally believe we have self-consciousness, (that is a state of being conscious of what we are) but we are deceiving ourselves because we are merely in a state where we arbitrarily, and erroneously, ascribe to ourselves qualities or attributes we do not have.

Thinking and Feeling...

According to Ouspensky, 'thinking' refers to the mental processes such as reasoning, compassion, affirmation, negation, speech, creativity and so on. He referred to 'feeling' or 'emotions' including joy and fear. He said that we cannot necessarily distinguish between thought and feeling, and tend to conflate the two.

I see this as insightful as it explains how your ProtoEgo by the feelings it elicits in you – which it often achieves by causing your body to secrete hormones (such as cortisol, norepinephrine, adrenalin or, say, dopamine) – directs your decision-making and establishes and reinforces your biases and your lack of consciousness.

As Ouspensky pointed out, this conflating of thought and feelings presents a major obstacle to discovering who you are and how you can evolve in consciousness.

Instincts...

Ouspensky said that we tend to use the words 'instincts' and 'instinctively' in the wrong sense. He said that we often use those words in relation to movement functions (that is, motor functions) such as walking and sometimes emotional behaviours; whereas he said there are only four classes of instinctive functions:

- First: there are the inner physiological functions of our bodies, such as breathing, digestion, blood circulation, body repair and so on

- Second: there are the so-called five senses (sight, hearing, smell, taste and touch), and senses such as weight, temperature, humidity, and so on
- Third: all the physical emotions, that is all the physical sensations that are either pleasant or unpleasant. This would include tastes, smells, bodily impacts (pleasant and unpleasant)
- Fourth: all motor reflexes, such as yawning, laughter and physical memories (such as of tastes, smells and memories of pain)

Ouspensky said we get confused about our terminology when, for example, we describe mechanical movements or functions as 'instinctive', such as catching a falling object without thinking that we should catch it.

He drew a distinction between inherent, unlearned, functions (such as breathing), which we can do from birth without having to learn them, and motor or cognitive functions such as walking or speaking a particular language, writing or drawing, all of which we must learn. Ouspensky's view was that anything we have to learn is not inherent and not instinctive.

The point Ouspensky makes is that all the functions we perform, even advanced functions such as writing or reading, do not equate to self-consciousness. In fact, they have nothing to do with the self or with consciousness. Such activities may involve perception, thought, orientation and even theorising, but they are not states of self-consciousness because they tell us nothing about the self; and, as I would put it, they leave the enemy of consciousness, the ego, intact.

As I see it, the point Ouspensky makes is valid and directly relevant to our ego intellect. Our ego intellect tells us, falsely, that we know who we are. This is a great self-deception and leads to erroneous theories such as the theory that our human origins lie in a spontaneous, non-divine, biological quirk that has been called 'evolution', and this error then leads to the erroneous conclusion that man has no soul and man's mortal life has no purpose.

What this means is that our ego intellects create a bubble of delusion in which we live; and unless we do something about it, we miss out on the biggest opportunity in the whole of Creation; an opportunity that comes to each of us, but only comes once.

Cognition of Truth...

Another way of appreciating this problem of our ego intellects creating a bubble of illusion that we mistake for being consciously aware is that it prevents us from being cognisant of truth. At best, with our egos at the helm, we can experience a relative truth; which, not being truth, is falsehood.

It's not until we achieve a true ego-less state of self-consciousness that we can begin to discern some level of truth about ourselves. My view is that this does not equate to us getting to and remaining above LoC 500 on David Hawkins' MoC as he suggested. In my view even at LoC 500 on Hawkins' MoC we're still the prisoners of our ego intellect with all its hubris, vanity, lies, self-delusion and deceptions; otherwise, we would be able to discern the purpose for human life – something Hawkins never figured out (*Power vs Force*, p314).

In what Ouspensky referred to as the fourth state of consciousness, objective consciousness, we begin to know the truth about things beyond ourselves. Hawkins would likely say that this starts at about LoC 540 on the MoC and grows logarithmically from there. Again, I disagree. To me truth can only be found via a humble heart. Without a humble heart to lead you your ego will take over.

We Lie to Ourselves... And Others...

A classic example of ego spirituality being present would be a professing Christian accepting the theory of a spontaneous, non-divine, biological origin and evolution of man (that is, Darwinism). These so-called Christians are living a lie. They're been led by their ego rather than a humble heart.

Ouspensky... Man's *Essence* and *Personality*...

Ouspensky's view was that man is born with *essence* and he develops or acquires *personality*. He said that essence cannot be lost but it can be subordinated below personality and thereby be spoiled. On the other hand, personality is always subject to change, depending on the circumstances, priorities or imperatives.

In today's language we might say that a person's personality may result from social and cultural conditioning, education and taught values, but that's not necessarily getting to the point that Ouspensky made.

He said that by nature man should like what is good for him and dislike what is bad for him, but that this natural harmony can only exist and be maintained as long as his essence is not subjugated by his personality.

When personality begins to dominate then, according to Ouspensky, man begins to act in ways and indulge in things that are contrary to his health and well-being; and he can even develop a morbid liking for, and even penchant for, harmful things.

Essence... Non-Ego... and Heart...

I agree with Ouspensky about essence and personality, although I would word it differently. As I see it, man is born in an ego-less state (what I believe Ouspensky refers to as 'essence'), but is socially conditioned to develop a personality, which I would say incorporates various manifestations of ego.

As I see it, in the non-ego state, which can be equated to a state of humility, man can far more easily discern truth; but he uses his ego-less heart, not his mind, to do so.

As I see it, once man is tainted by ego then at all times when his ego is in the driver's seat, he cannot engage an ego-less heart and cannot discern truth; or can only do so fortuitously.

To my way of thinking, an ego-less heart is far more powerful than an enormous intellect that is hamstrung by ego; or a high LoC on David Hawkins' MoC. The former can 'see' and the latter is 'blind'.

This is why I say that intellect is not a prerequisite for consciousness, because it's invariably tainted by ego. Until we learn to let our ego-less hearts counsel and guide our ego-full intellect we remain 'lost'. To use Ouspensky's terminology, I see an ego-less heart as our essence, and I see our intellect as a major part of our personality or ego identity; an identity built on falsehood and living by falsehoods.

What You Have Learned in This Chapter

- David Hawkins' MoC isn't complete or even necessarily reliable
- Whichever approach to the ego problem you take, you will discover one underlying theme, namely that whenever your ego is in charge you cannot find truth, because you're not looking for it

- Nonetheless, according to Hawkins, the more conscious you become the more apparent it becomes that the Darwinian concept of a spontaneous, non-divine, biological origin of man is false
- None of us can be complete while we're trapped by the notions of our ego intellect
- David Hawkins' MoC can't lead you to truth just as it failed to lead him to discern the purpose of his own life (*Power vs Force*, p314)

Chapter 12

Your Ego and Love... and Truth...

What You'll Discover in This Chapter...

- The ego's version of what is love, by which most people are guided, is flawed and failure prone, and that's because of what the ego is
- Love, in its truest sense, is neither emotional nor intellectual
- True love is all about truth and selflessness
- Your ego will always rail against true love, and against truth, because to accept them requires the dissolution of the ego in its current guise

Common Concepts of 'Love'...

'Love', as most people perceive and experience it, is an emotion, and nothing else. There are many other emotions, such as happiness, fear, anger, disgust, loathing and shame. Emotions are so powerful that they're often reflected in spontaneous, uncontrollable physiological signs: blushing, increased heart rate, gulping, tightness of breath, sweating, shaking or trembling.

Put simply, emotions are either pleasant (agreeable) or unpleasant (disagreeable) states of feeling that occur without conscious effort; but they can also be catalysts for unpredictable, irrational and harmful behaviour – and 'love', as human history shows, is no different.

Insight: If 'negative' intellectual concepts (such as fascism, communism or jihadism) are bolstered by emotions (such as passion, or 'love' for the cause in question) they can become dangerous idealism. This is where the ProtoEgo is at its worst.

Interestingly, 'love' and faith or 'love' and belief often go hand-in-hand; but that's not the starting point for understanding what love is. Clive Staples Lewis

(1898-1963) was a Fellow and Tutor in English literature at Oxford University. In 1960, in his book *The Four Loves*, Lewis explored the nature of spiritual love.

Lewis drew a distinction between selfless love (referred to by him as 'agape love') and three other forms of 'love' he identified: affection, friendship and romantic love. Lewis said that the latter three differ from agape love in that they involve reciprocal benefit.

Agape love, on the other hand, is selfless. This selfless form of love, in which the person giving the love asks for nothing in return and may even suffer loss as a result of that love is something that the ego is simply not capable of.

What Is Love, Really...?

The greatest description of true love, self-effacing love, non-ego love, is found in the New Testament: 1 Corinthians 13:4-13.

Love is patient, love is kind. It does not envy [like ego does], *it does not boast* [like ego does], *it is not proud* [like ego is].

It does not dishonour others [like ego does], *it is not self-seeking* [like ego is], *it is not easily angered* [like ego is], *it keeps no record of wrongs* [like ego does].

Love does not delight in evil but rejoices with the truth.

It always protects, always trusts, always hopes, always perseveres.

Love never fails. But where there are prophecies, they will cease; where there are tongues, they will be stilled; where there is knowledge, it will pass away.

For we know in part and we prophesy in part,

but when completeness comes, what is in part disappears.

When I was a child [when I was driven by ego?], *I talked like a child, I thought like a child, I reasoned like a child. When I became a man, I put the ways of childhood* [ego?] *behind me.*

For now we see only a reflection as in a mirror; then we shall see face to face. Now I know in part [I do not, at present, know the truth]; *then I shall know fully, even as I am fully known.*

And now these three remain: faith, hope and love. But the greatest of these is love.

What's more, other verses of the New Testament tell us in effect that this ego-less love is a blessing not only for the receiver by also for the giver: in 1 Peter 4:8 we are told:

"And above all things have fervent love for one another [not love of ourselves], for love will cover a multitude of sins."

Whereas the ego is always fearful, 1 John 4:18 tells us:

"There is no fear in love, but perfect love casts out fear…"

Love will cover a multitude of sins (1 Peter 4:8). Love covers all wrongs (Proverbs 10:12). To 'cover' sin is to forgive it. Jesus commanded that we love one another (John 13:34-35). Love keeps no record of wrongs (1 Corinthians 13:5). So, if you cannot forgive others, you do not know and practice love.

True Love Requires the Dissolution of Ego…

When Jesus was asked: "Which is the first commandment of all?" (Mark 12:28-30), he answered:

"… and you shall love the Lord your God with all your heart, with all your soul, with all your mind and with all your strength. This is the first commandment. This is the first and great commandment. And the second is like it: You shall love your neighbour as yourself. There is no other commandment greater than these."

The Ego's Greatest Love Is Itself… It's Anthropocentric…

The ProtoEgo's role has always been to promote your survival, even if that could only be achieved at the cost of others. As other manifestations of the ego have emerged – such as the intellectual ego and the religious ego, which have come forward with the development of our limbic system and frontal lobe – the ProtoEgo has re-fashioned its role and its strategy.

The ProtoEgo has always been and always will be anthropocentric. The word anthropocentric is made up of 'anthropo', meaning man or human, and 'centric', meaning at the centre or pinnacle (indicating the belief that man or humans are the most important and valuable thing in the universe).

The problem is that humans have human nature, and at the centre of human nature is the selfish, grasping, greedy ego. So, if we are anthropocentric – as humanists are – we are building a very dangerous world for ourselves and our children.

Anthropocentrism Is the Ego's Disguise...

Your ego, like mine, is clever as well as devious. As your ego sees things it has to be clever and devious in order to save you from yourself; to save you from the hare-brained ideas, such as altruism, that your conscious frontal lobe, or your heart, dreams up. After all, how can your ego guarantee your survival if you're being altruistic.

So, your ego cleverly outwits you by getting you to believe that the thing to be cherished most in the entire universe is human life – by which it really means the ego's version of what human life is. In other words, anthropocentrism and humanism are dangerous.

Wisdom Does not Promote Humanism or Anthropocentrism...

As I pointed out earlier, the teachings of Jesus set, first, God and secondly, your fellow man – not yourself – at the centre and pinnacle of all things, with God always being first.

I'm not trying to convert you to Christianity by making these comments. I'm merely trying to shine light on your ego so you can see it more clearly and can make choices that reflect a deeper, universal truth; which begs the questions: Does truth exist? What is truth?

Truth and the Ego's Love of Relativism...

Relativism, like humanism and anthropocentrism, is another dangerous ego endorsed deception. Relativism is the belief, or propaganda, that there is no universal truth about anything – it's a dog-eat-dog free-for-all. Relativism fits in nicely with the Darwinian theory of a spontaneous, non-divine biological evolution of humankind; another ProtoEgo endorsed deception, another ticking time bomb.

What Is Truth and Where can it be Found...?

Truth emanates not from man but from creation; and that's scientific fact, whether science realises it or not.

Truth cannot emanate from man because man's 'reality' is perceived, man's 'reality' is a product of the subconscious signature filtering and behavioural programmes we have contrived for survival in our ego-dominated, and therefore hostile world; a Darwinian dystopia that is devoid of love and blighted by ego-love. This cannot change, cannot improve, while mankind is the prisoner of ego; because the ego's primary quality is perception, not truth.

The real problem with anthropocentricity is that each group of humans holds their values above those of the conflicting values of any other group and will value themselves above other groups; leading to distrust, disliking, rivalry and inevitable conflict at one or more levels.

The persistence of our ego in its troublesome form condemns mankind to division arising from differing realities and differing values. As individuals, it condemns us to inner conflict and bad outcomes in life.

To your ego, being 'right' is more important than being correct... more important than truth...

The simple fact is that your unbridled ego is less interested in truth than it is in being 'right' and proving all viewpoints other than its own to be 'wrong'. To admit that you're wrong requires humility, something that is foreign to the ego. In other words, at the heart of ego is vanity and pride; both of which lead to positionality, polarity and conflict.

Ego Viruses: Humanism, Relativism, Solipsism, Anthropocentrism...

It's not difficult to see that the often lauded, and now politically correct, position of humanism is really a facade for ego-relativism and solipsism. Its fruits are division and conflict because unless and until humans share and practice the same core truth and values there can only be conflict.

So, what we need to explore at some point is where do our (yours and mine) practised values come from, are they the right values, and how do we deal with the problem that our perception isn't reality or truth. That would lead us deeper into the world of Spiral Dynamics which is, unfortunately, outside the scope of this book; but we will get some snippets of that subject.

What You Have Learned in This Chapter

- The ego does not know truth or love

- Humanism and anthropocentrism are superficially enticing but are in fact dangerous and deadly
- To have peace and prosperity for ourselves and for others we need a core truth and core values that are true to creation, not ProtoEgo driven

Chapter 13

Man Learns Probability... but Doesn't Get Prophecy... and Decides to Become a Machine...

What You'll Discover in This Chapter...

- Real science shows that God exists and the Christian scripture is real
- Artificial intelligence will never be our future
- Christian scriptural prophecy is real

Are man's science and God's laws compatible? In order to fit in with God's master plan are we required to shun science, wear sackcloth, live in a tent in the wilderness and write with charcoal on animal hides or parchment? Is it possible for a leading-edge scientist not to be a de facto opponent of God?

There's nothing wrong with science *per se*. Science can be at one with God's laws without us 'losing' anything other than our egos, but there are a number of elementary principles, from the Christian spiritual standpoint, that we need to bear in mind in relation to science. I deal with some of these below.

Let's Look at Some Science from the Scripture...

The Christian scripture is unique among belief systems, in that it long ago revealed many things that are today classified by us as 'scientific', which were only much later 'discovered' by man. At the time these snippets of information were slipped into the scripture (by our Creator, through His servants and prophets) the significance of the information (at least from a *scientific* standpoint) probably didn't register with anyone. For example:

- That the Earth is round was revealed 2700 years ago (Isaiah 40:22)
- It's also clear that Jesus knew that the Earth was a sphere with different time zones – refer to Luke 17:34-36. These verses tell us that Jesus must have known that the Earth rotates and revolves around the sun and has different time zones
- There's the revelation of the hydrological cycle revealed 2900 years ago (Ecclesiastes 1:7)
- There's the startling revelation of the importance of blood to life revealed 3400 years ago (Leviticus 17:11)
- It was revealed 3400 year ago that circumcision for males has significant health benefits. We now know that male circumcision reduces dramatically the risks of cervical cancer in women, and God prescribed circumcision as a requirement for Old Testament marriage (Genesis 34:1-24)
- Recent 'discoveries' by science also substantiate that the eighth day after birth (the time decreed by God 2000 years ago: Luke 1:59) is exactly the right time (due to the composition of the blood at that point) for circumcision to be performed

God Rolls the Dice and Gives Man Intellect...

Knowing full-well that, after the Fall (Adam and Eve), our ego-driven anthropocentric leanings would cause man to forget God and use his magnificent intellect (which is a gift from God) to try to exert a form of control over his fellows, over our world – and beyond – God openly challenged us to unravel the mysteries of His Creation.

Here's what God said, knowing we'd throw up the likes of Richard Dawkins (*The God Delusion*) and Yuval Harari (*Homo Deus*):

"Let them bring out, and declare to us the things that shall happen [that is, let's see them prophesy the future – let's see them tell history in advance]; let them reveal the former things what they are [how the universe came about, the universe's history], that we may consider them, and know the final end of them; or declare to us the things to come [that is, foretell the end]. Reveal the things that are to come after this, so that we may know that you are gods [... *Homo Deus*...?]. Yea, do good or do evil so that we may be dismayed and see it together. Behold you are of nothing, and your work is of nothing. He who chooses you [in preference to God's word] is an abomination" (Isaiah 41:22-24).

Was God telling us by this scripture that He hates science, that He hates scientists and that He wants us to live in the stone age? The answer is: no. However, God is trying to prevail upon us to get our priorities right. We are told by God that we must *first* seek the Kingdom of God (Matthew 6:33), and not be side-tracked by our intellectual egos.

What Is Our Mortal Purpose...?

The reason God tells us this is because He is trying to drive home to us that there is a *specific* purpose for our mortal existence; namely so that we can be road-tested by Him, here on Earth, to ascertain whether we qualify for eternal life in His kingdom as part of His family. In order to satisfy the road-test we need to choose to first seek God's kingdom. That has to be our first priority. If we do not do that then, no matter what else we achieve in our human lives (whether it be amazing scientific discoveries or building great civilisations), it amounts to nothing because it will be ephemeral and we will not enter God's kingdom; our mortal lives will have been wasted.

God's Prophecies... A Huge Clue to the Existence of God...

God is also telling us by this scripture that:

- He can prophesy and determine the future – something that mortal man will never be able to do so – and He has long ago done it by His prophets in the scripture
- only He knows the history of our universe and only He can comprehend it, that mortal man will never be able to do so
- we are not gods, we will never be gods and we should not strive to be gods in our mortal state or otherwise – so don't have regard to the notions of the likes of Yuval Harari (*Homo Deus*) or the 'humanoid' artificial intelligence (AI) proponents

Man Can't Survive Guided by His Ego...

Without God's guidance, man would (as a result of his ego-driven anthropocentric outlook) despoil this planet and destroy himself. In other words, ego-driven humans will never be able to live in peace or abundance, because we will continue to follow the anthropocentric model for human behaviour that's been the source of human misery throughout ego history. This is no accident. It's designed to be so by our Creator, because He's trying to send us a message.

God has a master plan for all His creation. It's been in place for tens if not hundreds or thousands of millennia – since before He created us – and it will unfold His way no matter what man does. Nothing we do will alter the outcome. At worst, our personal choices will merely result in us, personally, being denied any role in God's eternal kingdom.

Man's Science Is Unreliable…

What we know about the natural world is derived from experiences in the natural world, which is an infinitesimally tiny part of God's creation; and those experiences are derived through our senses. There is nothing absolute about our scientific knowledge.

Science will never be reliable or certain, even when it comes to physics. Our scientific knowledge espouses laws that are descriptive, not absolute or prescriptive. They do not tell us what Creation is, how it came about, how it operates or what its future is. They merely describe what the natural creation seems to be like, a perception.

Man's Science Doesn't Make Sense… Even to Scientists…

Consider the following discrepancies with man's science.

Seth Lloyd Discovers… Nothing…

Mainstream science says that matter can neither be created nor destroyed. However, Professor Seth Lloyd (Professor of Mechanical Engineering at MIT, principal investigator at the Research Laboratory of Electronics, designer of the first feasible quantum computer) stated in his book *Programming the Universe* (Vintage Books, a division of Random House, 2007) that before the universe began there was 'nothing' (p45).

Seth says that there was: "Not just empty space, but the absence of space itself" (p45).

He says: "Before the Big Bang, there was nothing, no energy, no bits… Then, all at once, the universe sprang into existence. Time began, and with it, space."

How can this be so when man's science says that matter can neither be created nor destroyed? How could we have a 'Big Bang' from nothing?

The Evolutionists Attack Creation...

Secondly, despite the fact that the *theory* of the spontaneous, non-divine biological origin and evolution of man has not progressed from being a *theory* of science to a *law* of science in the 150 years since Darwin first dreamt it up, we are, nonetheless, subjected to the vitriolic, emotive outpourings of the bellicose champions of this theory of evolution, such as Richard Dawkins (*The God Delusion*), who stamp their feet, like petulant children, at the thought of a divine creation.

Other evolutionists have been more honest, up to a point. The biologist Richard Lewontin (*Billions and Billions of Demons*, New York Review of Books, 19 January 1997 (p31) said: "We take the side of science in spite of the patent absurdity of some of its constructs, in spite of the tolerance of the scientific community for unsubstantiated just-so stories, because we have a prior commitment, a commitment to materialism...we, cannot allow a Divine Foot in the door."

A Spontaneous, Non-Divine, Biological Origin and Evolution of Man Is a Fairy Tale...

Thirdly, despite the strident proclamations of the likes of Richard Dawkins true scientists know that the theory of man's spontaneous, non-divine biological origin and evolution is highly questionable.

For example, George Wald (former Professor, Harvard University) said, in the August 1954 edition of *Scientific American,* in an article "The Origin of Life": "The reasonable view is to believe in spontaneous generation; the only alternative is to believe in a single primary act of supernatural creation. There is no third position. One has only to contemplate the magnitude of this task to concede that the spontaneous generation of a living organism is impossible. Yet, here we are as a result, I believe, of spontaneous generation."

George Wald was more honest than Dawkins, yet he still had the flaw that many scientists have; namely, his intellectual ego would not allow him to embrace the truth (the existence of a Creator) in spite of the overwhelming scientific imperative. Nothing has changed, scientifically, since Professor Wald made the abovementioned statement.

If anything, the further science has gone the more cracks have appeared in the facade of the story of the spontaneous, non-divine biological evolution of man; including the evidence that makes up the concept of irreducible complexity, but mainstream science remains in denial of a Creator. Man's ego intellect is on steroids.

Man's Maths Don't Add Up...

Science is against the scientists when it comes to 'proving', by man's science or mathematics, the existence or non-existence of God. The way science usually tests such things is with the mathematical theory of probability; which is used world-wide on a daily basis (in mathematics, statistics, finance, commodities trading, the stock market, artificial intelligence/machine learning, demographics and gambling) to draw conclusions about the likelihood of potential events occurring.

There's no single accepted mathematical definition of 'probability'. However, that little fact doesn't really matter for my purposes, just as it doesn't matter for the governments and businesses around the world that use probability and statistics every day. For the purpose of coming to grips with the ego intellect what I'm interested in is how probability theory has been used to test Christian scriptural prophecy. I'm interested in this because:

- Christian scripture is unique in that about twenty-five per cent is prophecy. Prophecy is 'history told in advance'. In that sense, prophecy is (according to scriptural Christians) absolutely certain, whereas man's perceptions, man's predictions and man's forecasts are uncertain
- Some Christian scriptural prophecy not only gives details of events and identifies the places where those events will occur but often gives the duration of those events
- Some of the prophecy is even more specific than this – by giving us time-frame clues from which we can calculate the precise years or milestones when these prophesied events should have occurred
- There are hundreds of prophesied events referred to in the Christian scripture that have unfolded exactly as prophesied

According to man's science we can use probability theory to test whether Christian scripture and God are credible. This isn't difficult for man the mathematician because we know from resulting historical records whether the prophecies were fulfilled. Therefore, we can gauge the credibility of the Christian scripture by using probability theory to determine what the scientific likelihood is of every one of those prophesied events having been fulfilled as prophesied. In other words, we can test the credibility of the scripture.

Evidence From Christian Scriptural Prophesy...

Following is a list of more than 100 Old Testament scriptural prophecies concerning the Messiah; all of which were fulfilled by Jesus, to the letter.

Genesis	8 Prophecies
Exodus	3 Prophecies
Leviticus	1 Prophecy
Numbers	3 Prophecies
Deuteronomy	3 Prophecies
2 Samuel	2 Prophecies
1 Chronicles	2 Prophecies
Psalms	28 Prophecies
Isaiah	34 Prophecies
Jeremiah	9 Prophecies
Ezekial	5 Prophecies
Daniel	3 Prophecies
Hosea	1 Prophecy
Joel	1 Prophecy
Amos	1 Prophecy
Jonah	1 Prophecy
Micah	4 Prophecies
Zechariah	4 Prophecies
Malachi	2 Prophecies
Total	115 Prophecies

Mathematician Peter W. Stoner Crunched the Numbers...

No discussion of probability theory and Christian scriptural prophecy would be complete without referring to the milestone work of Peter W. Stoner (1888-1980), Chairman of the Departments of Mathematics and Astronomy at Pasadena City College until 1953; Chairman of the Science Division, Westmont College (1953-1957); Professor Emeritus of Science, Westmont College; Professor Emeritus of Mathematics and Astronomy, Pasadena City College.

In 1952, Professor Stoner co-published his ground-breaking book *SCIENCE SPEAKS, SCIENTIFIC PROOF OF THE ACCURACY OF PROPHECY AND THE BIBLE*, with Robert C. Newman, S.T.M., PhD; PhD in Astrophysics, Cornell University (1967); S.T.M., Biblical School of Theology (1972),

150

Associate Professor of Physics and Mathematics, Shelton College (1968-1971); Associate Professor of New Testament, Biblical School of Theology.

SCIENCE SPEAKS was reviewed by a committee of the American Scientific Affiliation (and its Executive Council) and was found to be accurate and reliable in its presentation of scientific material. In particular, the mathematical analysis used by Professor Stoner was found to be based on principles of probability that are considered thoroughly sound in science and which had been properly applied by him.

A number of important findings are referred to by the authors of *SCIENCE SPEAKS* including:

- In the decades prior to 1952, there were perceived to be discrepancies between the Old Testament book of Genesis (Chapter 1) and the findings of science, particularly in the field of astronomy. However, subsequent astronomical discoveries verified the Genesis account – yes, the modern science of astronomy corroborates the Book of Genesis (which was written 3,500 years ago)
- The chronology given in Genesis for the creation events correspond, in sequence, precisely with what modern science has subsequently discovered
- Bearing in mind that Moses wrote Genesis 3,500 years ago the chances of him considering all the components that made up the creation is mind-boggling. According to Professor Stoner, Moses had only one chance in 311,351,040 of getting it right – but he managed to do so
- Professor Stoner also says that it was one thing for Moses to identify the components of the creation – an incredible feat in itself – but it was another for him to get them in the correct sequence. Professor Stoner put Moses' chances of doing this correctly at 1 in 31,135,104,000,000,000,000,000 – yet he did so

To put this in a context that we can understand, Professor Stoner gives an example. Suppose we decide to have a raffle and we print the number of tickets referred to above, to represent the number of chances. To get them printed we use eight million printing presses which each print two thousand tickets per minute, requiring them to run twenty-four hours a day for five million years. We mark one ticket and leave all the others blank, and then mix them up. We then blindfold a person and get him to try to draw out the solitary marked ticket. Professor Stoner says that the blindfolded person's chances of selecting the marked ticket are actually higher than Moses' chances of having guessed both the components and the sequence of the components of creation in order for him to write Genesis.

Professor Stoner points out that if we printed all the above-mentioned tickets (at a mere centimetre square, from stock that gives one hundred tickets a thickness of only one inch) then those tickets would cover the whole of North America from Canada through the USA to Mexico, from the Atlantic to the Pacific, one mile (1,609 m) deep.

The conclusion one must draw is that Moses, like all the other writers of the scripture, was inspired by God to write what he wrote; and we're told as much in the New Testament: "All Scripture [that is, including the Old Testament] is God-breathed and is profitable doctrine, for conviction, for correction, for instruction in righteousness; so that the man of God may be complete, fully equipped for every good work" (2 Timothy 3:16-17).

- The prophecies written in the Old Testament book of Ezekiel 26:3-5, 7, 12, 14, 16 (written in about 590 BC), concerning the destruction of the City of Tyre is another example. The probability of the fulfilment of each part of the prophecy, and having it all come true, was calculated by Professor Stoner at one in seventy-five million – yet they all came true, to the last detail
- In the Old Testament book of Micah 1:6-16 (written about 700 BC) the Prophet speaks of what will befall Samaria, which was still a prominent city seven-hundred-and-fifty years later in the time of Christ. Yet, in fulfilment of the prophecy, the city was reduced to a heap of stones. The chances of Micah prophesying the destruction of this great walled city, that it would lie in a heap of rubble rather than be rebuilt, that it would become a place of vineyards, that the stones from the city would be rolled down the hill (rather than being heaped together or used for rebuilding), that the makers of the gardens would dig down and remove all the foundation stones as well as surface debris, was estimated by Professor Stoner at one in forty thousand – yet it all happened as written
- Professor Stoner deals with similar Old Testament prophecies in relation to Gaza and Ashkelon, Jericho, the famous Golden Gate of Jerusalem,

Moab and Ammon, Edom and Babylon; and concludes that the probability of each of these prophecies coming true (calculated by multiplying all of the probabilities together) gives a figure of 1 in 5.76 x 10^{59} – yet they all occurred as written

To visualise what this figure means Professor Stoner suggests that we imagine we have the same number of silver dollars. The volume of those dollars would be more than a million times that of the earth, and were we to make these silver dollars into balls we would end up with 10^{28} solid silver balls the size of the sun

- Professor Stoner also considered the probability of Jesus fulfilling the eight prophetic events referred to in the following Old Testament scriptures:
  o (Old Testament) Micah 5.2 – that Jesus would come from Bethlehem Eprathah, estimated by Professor Stoner's at 2.8 x 10^5
  o (Old Testament) Malachi 3:1, concerning the sending of John the Baptist to prepare the way for Jesus, estimated by Professor Stoner at one in ten thousand
  o (Old Testament) Zechariah 9:9, concerning Jesus entering Jerusalem riding a colt (foal) of an ass, estimated by Professor Stoner at one in one hundred thousand
  o (Old Testament) Zechariah 13:6, concerning the betrayal of Jesus by Judas, resulting in Jesus' suffering, conservatively estimated by Professor Stoner at one in ten thousand
  o (Old Testament) Zechariah 11:12, concerning the thirty pieces of silver, conservatively estimated by Professor Stoner at one in ten thousand
  o (Old Testament) Zechariah 11:13, concerning the prophecy that the thirty pieces of silver would not be returned, conservatively estimated by Professor Stoner at 1 in 10^5
  o (Old Testament) Isaiah 53:7, concerning the affliction of Jesus, conservatively estimated by Professor Stoner at 1 in 10^4
  o (Old Testament) the prophesy referred to in Psalm 22:16 (concerning the piercing of Jesus' hands and feet) conservatively estimated by Professor Stoner at 1 in 10^4

When Professor Stoner multiplied out the probabilities for the abovementioned eight prophecies, he came to a probability of 1 in 10^{28} that one person could have fulfilled just these eight prophecies (all of which were fulfilled by Jesus).

Professor Stoner noted that the chances of any one man having lived after the day of the making of those prophecies down to the precise time that they were to be fulfilled (2,700 years) and all eight being fulfilled by that one man in his lifetime can be gleaned by dividing the figure 10^{28} by the total number of people who have lived since the time the prophecies were written. He worked on the basis that the best information available indicated that the number of people who lived from the time of the prophecies was eighty-eight billion. He then simplified the figures and came to the mathematical result that the chances of any one man out of those eighty-eight billion fulfilling all eight of the prophecies would be conservatively speaking, 10^{17}

- Professor Stoner noted that more than three hundred prophecies from the Old Testament dealing with first advent of Christ have been fulfilled and that the chances of one man fulfilling only sixteen of them is 1 in 10^{45}
- Professor Stoner says that to visualise this imagine taking that many silver dollars and making them into a solid ball, which gives you a sphere with a centre at the earth and extending in all directions more than thirty times as far as from the earth to the sun. Then put a mark on one of the silver dollars and stir up the ball, blindfold a man and ask him to try and pick out the marked dollar – now you have the extraordinary improbability of such events occurring unless guided by a divine mind and hand
- Then Professor Stoner considered the possibility of one human fulfilling forty-eight of the prophecies that were fulfilled by Jesus and came to the mathematical figure of 1 in 10^{157}.

Professor Stoner says to visualise this imagine taking electrons and laying them side by side to make a line one inch long. Were we to count the electrons in this line at the rate of 250 per minute (counting twenty-four hours a day) it would take 19 million years to do so. He then says that if we had a cubic inch of those electrons and tried to count them, it would take us 1.2×10^{38} years (2×10^{28} $\times$ 6 billion years back to the creation of the solar system).

So Why are so Many Scientists in Denial About God...?

Based on the abovementioned scientific investigation, it is perplexing to realise that most scientists apparently do not accept the Christian scripture. However, given that they cannot attack the mathematics used by Professor Stoner (they have no choice but to accept his work as being absolutely correct) what arguments do they use to try to discredit the scriptures?

Some atheists (and even mathematicians) attempt, in desperation, to discount or discredit the scriptures by asserting that particular events referred to in the Bible didn't occur or that particular people referred to in the Bible didn't exist. For example:

- Some have disputed that Jesus was crucified. However, the Roman historian Tacitus, who wrote of Nero's persecution of Christians in about 60 AD, also wrote of the crucifixion of Christ at the hands of the Pontius Pilate during the reign of the emperor Tiberius
- Some have asserted that Pontius Pilate never existed, but in 1961 a block of stone (now in the Israel Museum, Jerusalem, AE 1963 no. 104) has a carved inscription 'Tiberius Pontius, Prefect of Judah'.

The Old Testament Book of Daniel...

Probably the most compelling scriptural prophecies from the Old Testament are, however, the prophesies referred to in the Book of Daniel, concerning Jesus.

But before we go into that it is worthwhile mentioning the 'Rabbinic Curse' referred to in Talmudic Law (Sanhedrin 97b) which states: "May the bones of the hands and the bones of the fingers decay and decompose of him who turns the pages of the Book of Daniel to find out the time of Daniel 9:24-27, and may his memory rot from off the face of the earth forever."

The reason some practitioners of Judaism are apparently so concerned about chapter 9 of the Book of Daniel is that it was written in the late 6th century BC (five hundred years before Jesus was born) but it gives us information which enables us to *precisely* calculate the year of the Messiah's (Jesus') first coming.

The leaders of Judaism realised that if their congregations were aware of this, they would realise that the Messiah had already come and that their belief system (Judaism) – at least to the extent that it denies that Jesus was the Messiah – is flawed.

The clues that come from Daniel chapter 9 are as follows:

- Verse 24 – Daniel was inspired to write that seventy weeks are decreed upon 'your people' (that is, the inhabitants of the Kingdom of Judah – the descendants of the tribe of Judah, tribe of Benjamin and some of the tribe of Levi) and for your holy city (Jerusalem) "…to finish the transgression and to make an end of the sin, and to make reconciliation for iniquity, and bring in everlasting righteousness, and to seal up the vision and prophesy, and to anoint the Most Holy"

Insight: We know that in the case of prophecy a day is to be equated to a year and a week is to be equated to seven years (Ezekiel 4:6 and Numbers 14:34)

- Verse 25 – Daniel was inspired to write that from the time of the commandment to restore and to build Jerusalem until the coming of the Messiah shall be seven weeks and sixty-two weeks. This was telling Daniel that (69 weeks x 7 = 483 years) would pass between the time of the commandment to restore and build Jerusalem until the coming of the Messiah
- Verse 26 – after sixty-two weeks (434 years) the Messiah would be 'cut off'.
- Verses 13-14 – Daniel had a vision of hearing one holy person speaking with another and the first asks: How long shall the vision last concerning the daily sacrifice and the transgression that causes desolation, to give both the sanctuary and the host to be trampled underfoot? The second answers that it will be two thousand three hundred days (that is, 2300 years)
- Depicting this information diagrammatically, we come up with the following:

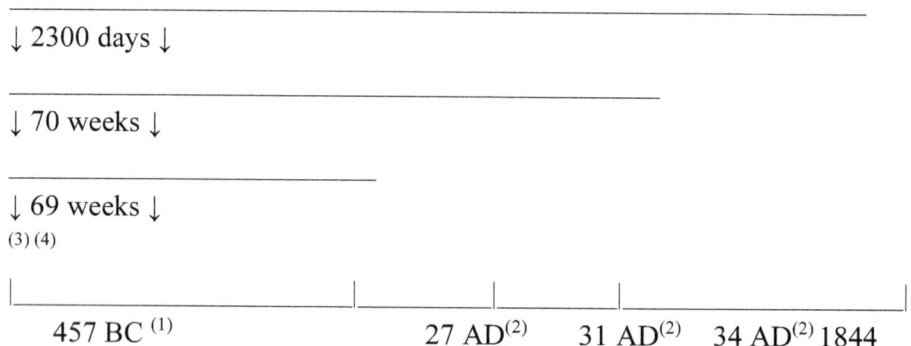

1) Artaxerxes decree to restore and rebuild Jerusalem
2) 7 days (years) duration
3) mid-point 3.5 days (years)
4) Stephen killed (that is, Jesus' followers are also rejected by the Jews)

The following points need to be noted concerning the prophecy and its depiction in this diagram:

o   Artaxerxes decreed that Jerusalem shall be restored and rebuilt in the year 457 BC
o   sixty-nine weeks (483 years) later, in 27AD, Jesus was baptised and commenced His ministry, which lasted three-and-a-half years

As stated in Daniel 9:26-27, the Messiah was to be 'cut off' after sixty-two weeks, (62 x 7 = 434 years) having made a firm covenant with many for one week (seven years); in the middle of which (at the three-and-a-half-year point) "…He shall cause the sacrifice and the offering to cease" [referring to the sacrifices God had required, prior to Jesus' crucifixion, from the Israelites].

In fulfilment of this, at the mid-way period between 27AD and 34 AD Jesus was crucified. The crucifixion took place in the spring of 31 AD, three-and-a-half years after His baptism.

In Matthew 10:6-7 we are told that Jesus commanded His disciples to go to the lost sheep of the house of Israel to tell them that the Kingdom of God was at hand. He was telling them to go back to the Jews and tell them what was about to happen. In accordance with this Stephen went back to preach the gospel to the Jews (Acts 6:8-10). The Jews stoned Stephen to death (Acts 7:58).

Significantly, a young man called Saul (later to be the apostle Paul) stood by to guard the coats of the stone-throwers. Saul subsequently persecuted Christians (Acts 8:1-3) but came to understand the truth whilst on his way to Damascus to persecute others (Acts 9:3-5). He was instructed by God to proceed into Damascus where he subsequently preached the gospel in the synagogue.

What this means is the seven-year covenant made by Jesus with His followers (as per Daniel's prophecy written five centuries earlier) came to an end in 34 AD with the death of Stephen. From that point in time, the house of the Jews (the deniers of Jesus as the Messiah) was left 'desolate' (Matthew 23:38).

The 'gospel' (meaning 'good news') was then directed towards the Gentiles (that is, those who did not practice Judaism) (Acts 13:46-47) because the Jews had rejected the gospel by rejecting Jesus.

Plainly, the Scriptural Prophecy Is Correct...

The above tells us that, measured on the benchmark of man's theory of probability, God and Jesus exist and the scriptures are to be believed.

Today's Scientists Who Deny God are no Different from The Jews Who Denied Jesus...

However, rather than accept their own science as proof of their Creator, their Saviour and the truth of the scriptures, our scientists go their own anthropocentric, humanist way.

One would think that having used their science (Professor Stoner's work using probability theory) to show that God is real, that the scriptures are inspired of God (and that we should be studying God's plans for us rather than our idiotic plans for space travel and 'humanoid' AI) scientists would be less concerned with trying to discredit God and the scripture and would, instead, embrace them.

Yet, Scientists Reject not Only God... They also Reject Man...

Many scientists not only reject God they also seem to reject man. I say this because they think they can create smarter-than-human intelligence in 'humanoids' and they plan to do so. This field of 'study' is given the name 'The Singularity'. The term is defined to mean 'the moment when technological change becomes so rapid and profound, it represents a rupture in the fabric of human history.'

In February 2011, *Time* magazine, in an article entitled 'THE SINGULARITY IS NEAR', (the title to the article having been taken from the title of a book written by Raymond Kurzweil, in 2005) one Vernor Vinge (a science-fiction novelist) is quoted as saying: "Within thirty years, we will have the means to create superhuman intelligence. Shortly after, the human era will be ended."

Vernor's article shows you how off the rails man's ego intellect can get.

But some scientists are in raptures; dreaming of a computer that is itself a scientist (that is, a machine built in their image); far more advanced than its slower-thinking human creator, able to work incredibly quickly; effortlessly drawing on huge amounts of data, and not requiring any rest breaks.

These nutter scientists are already talking of humans 'merging' with these computers to become super intelligent cyborgs, with the side-benefit of indefinite life-spans.

Vernor's article says: "The one thing all these theories have in common is the transformation of our species into something that is no longer recognisable as such to humanity circa 2011."

This is ego insanity.

What's more, these scientists are already saying of the singularity that: "… it's a serious hypotheses about the future of life on earth."

Indeed, the article mentions the then three-year-old Singularity University, which offers inter-disciplinary courses of study for graduate students and executives. The institution is hosted by NASA, and Google was a founding sponsor.

Raymond Kurzweil has apparently made two documentaries, one of which is called *The Transcendent Man*. Kurzweil predicted back in the early 2000, that scientists will successfully reverse-engineer the human brain by the mid-2020s. He has predicted that by 2030 computers will be capable of human-level intelligence. He puts the date of achieving the singularity at 2045; at which time he estimates that given the vast increases in computer power and corresponding reductions in costs, the quantity of artificial intelligence being created will be about a billion times the sum of all the human intelligence that existed in 2011.

Besides the Singularity University there is also a Singularity Institute for Artificial Intelligence based in San Francisco. One of its advisors is Peter Thiel (a former CEO of PayPal). The institute holds an annual conference called the Singularity Summit.

The abovementioned *Time* article says that at the 2010 Singularity Summit (San Francisco) there were, besides computer scientists, psychologists, neuro-scientists, nanotechnologists, molecular biologists, a specialist in wearable computers, a professor of emergency medicine, an expert on cognition in grey parrots and countless others.

The *Time* article says that after artificial intelligence the most talked-about topic was life extension. It seems that the biological boundaries that most people think of as permanent and inevitable are considered by adherents to the singularity as being 'problems' that will be solved in the foreseeable future.

The *Time* article reports a British biomedical gerontologist Aubrey de Grey (Chief Science Officer of the SENS Research Foundation and Vice President of AgeX Therapeutics Inc.) as saying to the effect that people have begun to realise that the view of aging being something inevitable is ridiculous. He says the human body is a machine that has functions, and it accumulates various types of damage as a side effects of the normal function and one day scientists will find solutions to all these problems.

So, this scientist like so many others thinks that you and your loved ones are just soul-less 'machines', and he believes that medical technology will one day enable humans not to die of age-related causes.

The *Time* article says in relation to the idea of indefinitely expending human life that: "Kurzweil finds that life extension produces resistance in his audiences: 'There are people who can accept computers being more intelligent than people, but the idea of significant changes to human longevity – that seems to be particularly controversial. People invested a lot of personal effort into certain philosophies dealing with the issue of life and death. I mean, that's the major reason we have religion.'"

So, as far as Kurzweil is concerned the Christian scripture is just make believe.

What Would Machine Man Do...?

The opponents of the singularity have one concern, according to the *Time* article; namely what would a highly advanced artificial intelligence, finding itself newly created and inhabiting planet earth, choose to do? Would it be friend or foe?

The supporters of the singularity claim that one of the goals of the Singularity Institute is to make sure not just that artificial intelligence develops but also that the AI is friendly.

We can't even get people, nations, to be friendly, but they say they'll get AI machines to be our friends.

Yet, even among scientists, there are sceptics about the ability of our scientists to bring about the singularity. For example, at the 2010 Singularity Summit the biologist Denis Bray said: "Although biological components act in ways that are comparable to those in electronic circuits, they are set apart by the huge number of different states they can adopt. Multiple bio-chemical processes create chemical modifications of protein molecules, further diversified by association with distinct structures at defining locations of a cell. The resultant combinatorial explosion of states in endows living systems with almost infinite capacity to store information regarding past and present conditions and a unique capacity to prepare for future events."

Bray was saying that this makes the ones and zeros that computers trade in look pretty crude; but Kurzweil and his faction disregard these challenges as being within the capacity of computer science to overcome.

Scientists Ditch Darwin...

The *Time* article says: "In Kurzweil's future, biotechnology and nanotechnology give us the power to manipulate our bodies and the world around us at will, at the molecular level... We ditch Darwin and take charge of our own evolution. The human genome becomes just so much code to be bug-tested and itemised, and, if necessary, rewritten. With indefinite life extension comes a reality; people die only if they choose to."

The belief is that we will ultimately, in effect, scan our consciousness into computers and enter a virtual existence or swap our bodies for immortal robots. The *Time* article says: "A hundred years from now, Kurzweil and de Grey and others could be the 22nd century's answer to the Founding Fathers "... except unlike the Founding Fathers, they'll still be alive to get the credit..."

The *Time* article states: "You may reject every specific article of the Singularitarian charter but you should admire Kurzweil for taking the future seriously. Singularitarism is grounded in the idea that change is real and humanity is in charge of its own fate and that history might not be as simple as one damn thing after another. Kurzweil loves to point out that your average cell phone is about a millionth the size of, a millionth the price of and a thousand times more powerful than the computer he had at MIT 40 years ago."

Kurzweil Is Mistaken...

Thankfully, in my belief, none of these sinister dreams of our scientists will ever come to fruition. There a number of reasons for this if you accept what the Christian scriptures say, for example:

- God expressly created man for a particular purpose. God has in mind to expand the God Family beyond God the Father and God the Son and will

161

give to those humans who meet His requirements eternal life in His kingdom. No human will ever have eternal mortal life

- This world as we know it is temporary. The way I read the scripture, planet Earth will be remade twice – once at the end of the Great Tribulation, and again at the end of the millennium following the short period (say, one hundred years) when Satan is loosed from the abyss in order to test those humans who will come up in the second resurrection (for the Great White Throne Judgment)

  After this, Satan will be finally defeated and the Earth will be remade (to remove every vestige of unlawfulness, unrighteousness, corruption and pollution) so that it will be fit to be inhabited by God the Father, along with God the Son and the extended God family

- God's plan has been in writing for humankind to read for thousands of years – in the Old Testament and the New Testament

- God has told us that we should not imagine for a moment that we have anything like His power or His knowledge; that what He says will come to pass will, indeed, come to pass:

"I am the Lord, that is My name; and My glory I will give to no other, nor My praise to carved images. Behold, the former things have come to pass, and new things I declare; before they spring forth I tell you of them." (Isaiah 42:8-9)

"To whom then will you liken Me, or to whom shall I be equal?" says the Holy One. Lift up your eyes on high and see how has created these things, who brings out their host by number; He calls them all by name, by the greatest of His might and by the strength of His power; not one is missing." (Isaiah 40:25-26)

The Creator's Unequivocal Message to the Created...

"Let them bring forth and show us what will happen; let them show the form of things; what they were, that we may consider them, and know the latter end of them; or declare to us things to come. Show the things that are to come hereafter, that we may know that you are God, yes do good or do evil that we may be dismayed and see it together. Indeed you are nothing, and your work is nothing; He who chooses you is an abomination." (Isaiah 41:22-24)

The Creator Will Determine the Future of HIs Creation...

God has stated that He will determine what occurs, no one else:

"Indeed I have spoken it; I will also bring it to pass. I have purposed it; I will also do it" (Isaiah 46:11).

The sooner all our egos realise this, the better.

God Isn't our Enemy...

God is not an enemy of man or of us acquiring knowledge. He is the enemy of untruth. He is the one that gave us our intellects and our ability to discover.

However, God also gave us His laws which He requires us to follow. It is more important to God that we follow His laws than achieve anything else in our worldly existence, including 'great' advances in science; because by following His laws you enhance your chances of receiving the eternal rewards He wants us all to enjoy.

From God's perspective (which is the only perspective that counts) our mortal lives are merely a road-testing stage for each of us to enable God to ascertain whether we will be admitted to eternal spiritual life in His Family. As far as God is concerned, it would make no difference whether we achieve all manner of amazing worldly achievements, such as achieving great scientific discoveries, if we fail to pass this test that He has set for us.

Bearing in mind the abovementioned points, it should be obvious to us that our science of artificial intelligence is an affront to God, is a rejection of God.

What You Learned in This Chapter...

- Our science strives to indefinitely extend human life (to make us 'immortal') but it will fail
- Left to their own devices our scientists would literally destroy human life
- Our 'humanoid' AI science is warped and dangerous and would lead to 'man' worshipping 'man'.

Chapter 14
Hawking Denies God... God Denies Hawking...

What You'll Discover in This Chapter...

- You will either accept or not accept God during your life – there is no neutral position
- Those who reject God appear generally to do so because their ego trips them up
- We have been given plenty on which to found our belief and faith in God so there won't be any excuses and no second chances, for you or anyone else
- The price for getting it wrong in this mortal life will be great, and will stand for eternity

After having read Chapter 13, in which the science of probability theory was used to plainly demonstrate that scientists should embrace the Christian scripture as incontrovertible and God as real, you would think that eminent scientists would be the first to acknowledge God, but that's not the case.

Given the probability results that Professor Stoner came up with in his detailed analysis of the fulfilled prophecies of the Christian scripture, one only needs to imagine, for a moment, what the likelihood is for our earth having come about, supporting its human and other life, in a non-divine, spontaneous 'accident' from a 'Big Bang' and you'll begin to laugh at how silly man's ideas can be.

Notwithstanding this, we get the likes of Stephen Hawking having the ego affrontery to pronounce that God doesn't exist.

Hawking's First Viewpoint...

In his book *A Brief History of Time from the Big Bang to Black Holes* (first published in 1988) Hawking attempts to explain a range of subjects in cosmology, including the so-called Big Bang, black holes and light cones, to non-scientists such as the author of this book. The book ends with a statement: "If we find [a unified theory], it would be the ultimate triumph – for then we would know the mind of God."

In effect, in his 1988 book, Hawking seemed to express the view that there is no incompatibility between the existence of a creator God and the scientific understanding of the universe.

Hawking's Change of Mind...

However, in his book *The Grand Design* (2010) Hawking says that "Modern science leaves no room for the existence of a creator God of the universe."

Which of Hawking's Perceived Conflicting Views Is Correct...?

Was Hawking right the first time (in his 1988 book); or was he right in 2010 when he said, in effect, that God doesn't exist?

In his 2010 book, Hawking claims that there is a new theory, the M-Theory, (where 'M' stands for 'membrane' or 'murky' or 'missing', depending upon one's particular version of the theory) which 'answers' all science's questions. In fact, the M-Theory is a re-run of what used to be known as the 'superstring' theory; with the string now becoming membranes. M-Theory is not a single theory but a number of theories about anything and everything you choose. Maybe the 'm' really stands for 'muddled'.

What Is Science About, Anyway...?

We need to understand that in man's science there are three levels of 'belief' or 'faith' in man's scientific ideas.

First, there's man's scientific 'hypothesis'. This is a so-called 'educated guess' based on observation. According to man's science, a hypothesis can be disproven but it cannot be proven to be true. It's supposedly a 'rational' explanation of a single event or phenomenon based on observation.

Second, there's man's scientific 'theory'. This is an explanation of a set of related observations or events based upon 'established' (whatever that means) hypotheses. According to man the scientist, when properly used, the term refers to an idea that can be tested and shown to be 'reliable', not *true*; but *reliable*, whatever that means.

Third, there's man's scientific 'law'. A scientific law is a statement of so-called fact meant to describe an action or set of actions. Man's scientific laws are supposedly true and universal. They are sometimes expressed by way of a mathematical equation. Scientific laws must apparently be simple, universal and unqualified to be accepted as true; because if a scientific law were to fail in any situation, then all science based on that law would collapse. Examples of scientific laws are the law of gravity, Boyle's law of gases and Hook's law of elasticity.

What this means (using the above three definitions) is that even by man the scientist's measure the string theories and M-Theories are unreliable as a basis for reaching a position on the subject at hand; namely the existence or non-existence of a creator God, because they're just theories.

And let's face it, how can you have 'an educated guess' (that is, a theory) that God doesn't exist merely because you haven't seen Him? The entire idea is idiotic.

There's no mathematical equation that can tell you whether or not God exists; or that can, for example, ever prove or disprove the Darwinian theory of the spontaneous, non-divine biological origin and evolution of humankind.

God's Warning to HIs Mockers... Like Stephen Hawking...

If you reject God, God will reject you: "Do not be deceived. God is not mocked; for whatever a man sows, that shall he also reap. For the one who sows to his own flesh shall reap corruption from the flesh. But the one who sows to the Spirit shall reap eternal life from the Spirit" (Galatians 6:7-8).

A Belated 'Sorry' Mightn't Cut it...

And bear in mind, belated changes of mind won't help you: "Not everyone who says to Me, *'Lord, Lord'*, shall enter into the kingdom of heaven; but the one who is doing the will of My Father, Who is in heaven" ... "And then I will confess to them, *'I never knew you. Depart from Me, you who work lawlessness'*" (Matthew 7:21, 23).

You'll be measured and judged by what you did and said during your life not by a belatedly death-bed apology.

Everyone Has to Front Up... You and me Included...

Each of us will answer: "...for the hour is coming in which all who are in the graves shall hear His voice and shall come forth: those who have practised good [that is, good as measured in God's eyes, not in man's eyes] unto a resurrection of life, and those who have practised evil [such as denying or denouncing God] unto a resurrection of judgment" (John 5:28-29).

Back to Professor Stoner...

I don't know about you, but for me the stakes are too high to let my ego flippantly decide that there's no Creator, no God; especially in light of, say, Professor Stoner's work on the compelling impact of scriptural prophecy.

So, What Happens to Hawking, Crick, Kurzweil, Harari and the Other Sceptics...?

There will be two judgments that will follow from the return of Christ. The first judgment is at the Judgment Seat of Christ (the 'Bema' seat), where those who believed and were righteous will be 'rewarded'. 1 Thessalonians 2:19-20. In those verses, the apostle Paul says to the effect that he drew courage from and was motivated by the knowledge that these rewards would follow.

In Revelation 22:12, Christ made it clear that when He returns, He brings with Him His reward to render to every man according to what he has done.

What this is telling us is that while grace and salvation (neither of which are on Hawkins' MoC) are gifts they are not all that the righteous will receive. They will also receive 'rewards', whereas those who were faithless, such as all non-believers (such as Hawking, Harari, Francis Crick, Raymond Kurzweil, and so on) will lose the opportunity for this inheritance; something that could have been theirs for eternity.

It's the choice of each of us whether we will subordinate our ego below our heart so that we can develop faith, and believe; and it's up to us to choose whether or not to practice living righteously and to what level.

Insight: The key verses of the scripture on rewards are Romans 14:10-11; 1 Corinthians 3:11-15; 2 Corinthians 5:9-10; 1 John 2:28 and Revelation 3:11-12. There's also no mention of rewards on Hawkins' MoC.

The Judgment Seat of Christ (Bema Seat)...

The apostle Paul said (referring to righteous believers) that they must all appear before the Judgment Seat of Christ to be judged according to what they did in their mortal, earthly lives (2 Corinthians 5:10; Romans 14:10, Ephesians 6:8).

Interestingly, it seems that this group may not include believers in God who lived and died before Christ; including Abraham, Isaac, Jacob (Israel), Noah, Moses, David, Daniel, and so on. They never were, and never could have been, Christians, because Christ came *after* them; so they may get a separate judgment; but even they knew that judgment, and rewards, awaited them (Psalm 62:12).

Those who are judged at the Judgment Seat of Christ will have already been forgiven their sins (Micah 7:19) because of their righteous faith. They will have eternal life in heaven; but their rewards will vary according to their works (1 Corinthians 3:15; 2 John 8; Micah 7:19, Romans 8:1; Galatians 3:13; 2 Corinthians 5:21; 1 John 2:28).

You can Either Gain or Lose Salvation... And Rewards...

The worst that can happen to those who are righteous believers is that they lose rewards that they could otherwise have had for eternity. This could happen if they worked less than they could have in developing and practising their righteousness. Speaking of God's gifts, the apostle Paul said (1 Corinthians 2:9-10, paraphrasing Isaiah 64:4):

"But it is written: *'Eye has not seen, nor ear heard, nor have entered into the heart of man the things which God has prepared for those who love Him. But God has revealed them to us through His Spirit. For the Spirit searches all things, yes, the deep things of God.'* "

The rewards for the righteous believers will be proportionate to their level of faithfulness (1 Corinthians 4:2; Luke 19:17-19; 2 Timothy 4:7).

Rejected God...? Don't Fret, You can Keep Your Ego...

There will be no reward for those who chose to reject God; but at least they'll have their egos to comfort them.

The Great White Throne Judgment Is Different...

Those who deny God lose salvation. Their mortal lives will have been a total waste. They will have squandered everything that they could have had. Their paltry, trifling works as mortal men (such as 'great' scientific discoveries or theories) will be less than dust; meaningless, forgotten.

These people do not get to participate in judgment at the Judgment Seat of Christ. There's a different judgment for them. Revelation 20:11-15 speaks of the Great White Throne Judgment where those who do not believe in Jesus Christ are judged (and some condemned); referring to those whose names are not written in the Book of Life – Hawking, Dawkins, Crick, Kurzweil, Harari...? This is the final judgment prior to the lost being cast into the lake of fire.

There's no Hiding from God...

The books that are opened (Revelation 20:12) contain a full record of everyone's deeds, good and bad; because God knows everything that has ever been said, done or even thought, and He will judge and deal with each accordingly (Psalm 28:4; 62:12; Romans 2:6; Revelation 2:23; 18:6, 22:12).

Insight: What you should aim for is to get your name in the Book of Life.

What You Have Learned in This Chapter...

- The price for getting it wrong when it comes to God is grave and eternal
- The prophecy of the scripture should be enough to persuade anyone who hears of it or reads it to verify and to accept it
- When it comes to God, we are talking of 'faith' which is a level of knowing that is beyond David Hawkins' MoC, and beyond paltry human intellect such as the intellect of Stephen Hawking
- Faith can only spring forth and grow in the nourishment of a humble, contrite heart – it can never spring forth from ego

Chapter 15

Evolutionists Deny God –
God Denies Evolutionists...

What You'll Discover in This Chapter...

- If you want to play the dangerous game of denying God you should at least look at all the evidence first
- Spontaneous, non-divine biological evolution is a 'pin the tail on the donkey' theory of men, and it seems to blind them from other views on life and creation

Man's 'Scientific' Theories, Hypothesis and 'Laws'...

In the previous chapter of this book, I looked briefly at Stephen Hawking and made the point that a scientific 'law' (as distinct from a scientific 'hypothesis' or a scientific 'theory') is a statement of fact meant to describe an action or set of actions.

I noted in that chapter that scientific laws are accepted by scientists as being not only true but *universal*.

It's self-evident that scientific 'laws' to be valid must not only be unqualified, but *must* be applied without exception, in *all* applications and *all* instances.

The reason for this is that were a scientific law to fail to apply in *any* instance then *all* the science based on that law must collapse.

An example of such a scientific law is the law of gravity; which, to this day, man's science doesn't really comprehend.

So, What About the *Theory* of Man's Spontaneous, Non-Divine Biological Origin and Evolution... And Thermodynamics...?

This brings us to an interesting issue in relation to the evolutionists' theory of man's spontaneous, non-divine, origin and biological evolution; namely that this theory of evolution contradicts the first and second scientific *laws* of thermodynamics; and the theory should, therefore, have been long ago thrown out by the scientific community. The reasoning is fairly simple:

- Used in its broadest sense the term 'evolution' theorises that all organisms (man included) have derived by gradual biological diversification from common ancestral forms of life, by innate processes of variation and selection, and that this has occurred in circumstances where those ancestral forms of life were originally derived by spontaneous generation from inanimate matter
- Therefore, evolution implies ever-increasing organisation and ever-increasing complexity in the universe – in effect, a doctrine of continuous creation by mutation
- However, man's first scientific law of thermodynamics is the law of energy conservation, which says that although energy can be converted from one form to another, the total amount of energy in the universe remains unchanged, because; according to man the scientist, *energy can be neither created nor destroyed*
- Further, man's second scientific law of thermodynamics is to the effect that although the total amount of energy that remains after it has been converted from one form to another remains unchanged the less is its capacity or tendency available for useful work

This means that applying man's first and second scientific laws of thermodynamics to any closed mechanical system in which work is being accomplished through energy conversion (such as the so-called process of spontaneous biological evolution) the 'entropy' increases – where entropy is a mathematical formulation of the non-availability of the energy of or for or within that system.

According to man the scientist, these two laws of thermodynamics are irrefutable in any field of science, bar none.

The fundamental and universal importance of these two laws has been emphasised from the time they became scientific laws. For example, Harvard Physicist P.W. Bridgman stated (*Reflections on Thermodynamics, American Scientist*, Vol. 41, October 1953, p549): "The two laws of thermodynamics are, I suppose, accepted by physicists as perhaps the most secure generalisations from experience that we have. The physicists do not hesitate to apply the two laws to any concrete physical situation in the confidence that nature will not let him down."

That being so, it is reasonable for us to ask: how long will factions within the science community (such as evolutionists) continue to try to dupe us? Surely it's time for them to accept that the laws of thermodynamics are fatal to their fairy tale of man's spontaneous, non-divine biological origin and evolution. It's time for them to be honest.

This is particularly so when the whole basis of what is termed 'uniformitarianism' – which I'll go into in a moment – must come under question when it is sought to be applied to what is stated in the scriptures.

A Warning to Scientists from God… Keep Your Egos in Check…

If you reject God (by for example saying man just evolved, that man wasn't created by God) then God will reject you: "Do not be deceived. God is not mocked; for whatever a man sows, that shall he also reap. For the one who sows to his own flesh shall reap corruption from the flesh. But the one who sows to the Spirit shall reap eternal life from the Spirit" (Galatians 6:7-8).

And don't try to make it good by saying 'sorry' it was my ego's fault: "Not everyone who says to Me, *'Lord, Lord'*, shall enter into the kingdom of heaven; but the one who is doing the will of My Father, Who is in heaven" … "And then I will confess to them, *'I never knew you. Depart from Me, you who work lawlessness'*" (Matthew 7:21, 23).

You will reap what you sow: "…for the hour is coming in which all who are in the graves shall hear His voice and shall come forth: those who have practised good [that is, good as measured in God's eyes not in man's eyes] unto a resurrection of life, and those who have practised evil unto a resurrection of judgment" (John 5:28-29).

Those who put their ego intellect ahead of faith in God's word will answer: "For they sow to the wind, and they shall reap the whirlwind. It has no stalk; the bud shall yield no meal; but if it does yield, strangers [that is, those who are estranged from God] shall swallow it up" (Hosea 8:7).

Now Let's Look at Uniformitarian Geology...

First, an acknowledgment: much of the technical data (up to 1960) referred to in this chapter is derived from the book *The Genesis Flood, THE BIBLICAL RECORD AND ITS SCIENTIFIC IMPLICATIONS* (1961, P & R Publishing, John C. Whitcomb and Henry M. Morris). I'll refer to this book as *The Genesis Flood*.

Uniformitarianism is man's 'scientific' theory (yes, another one) that baldly states that all *existing* or *present* or *contemporary* physical processes are sufficient to explain all *past* and present states of

- The astronomical universe
- The geological universe
- The biological universe

The first point to be made is that this principle of uniformity in *present* astronomical, geological and biological processes is not in conflict with the Christian scriptures (refer to Genesis 8:22).

However, there is conflict between the scripture and man's theory of uniformitarianism when the theory is sought to be applied in such a way as to deny the possibility of *past* or *future* suspensions or alterations of astronomical, geological or biological processes by a creator God; such as the Great Flood of Noah's day, used by God to punish a depraved population.

Most scientists want you to believe what they believe; that biblical events such as the Great Flood and the escape of the Israelites across the Red Sea during the Exodus are fairy tales. They 'need' you to believe them, not God, so that their ego intellects get reassured and they don't lie in bed at night fearful of what awaits them if they're wrong. They don't want to go down alone in the face of a wrathful Creator; they want your company for that trip.

In the philosophy [yes, it's a philosophy not real science] of naturalism, the uniformitarianist assumption is that the same natural laws and same natural processes that we experience and observe in the universe:

- Have *always* operated in the universe in the past
- Apply everywhere in the universe, and particularly on planet Earth

Uniformitarianism is often summed up in the catch-cry 'the present is the key to the past'.

Uniformitarianism has for well over a century been a key assumption of historical geology. This assumption stems from the imaginations of Scottish naturalists of the 18th and 19th centuries; principally Charles Lyell in his *Principles of Geology* (1830). By the way, Lyell was a lawyer, not a geologist. Those whose works Lyell principally relied on were William Smith (a surveyor), James Hutton (an agriculturalist) and John Playfair (a mathematician). In other words, the concept of uniformitarianism in geology is not the work of geologists.

The polemic of the assumption of uniformitarianism is the view that the earth was shaped by a series of sudden, short-term and violent events, rather than by God.

I've got nothing against geologists or geology. I make no criticisms of the fields of geology other than the uniformitarian field of *historical* geology. It's the interpretation of 'historical' geological data that is the issue for me – and for you.

The experiential, analytical geological sciences of mineralogy, petrology, geophysics, mining geology, petroleum geology, structural geology, seismology, geochemistry, marine geology, petrography, sedimentation and ground-water geology are plainly legitimate; they're valid branches of geology.

Likewise, I'm not having a go at the sciences of geomorphology and stratigraphy, except to the extent that they're relied on to support the assumption of uniformitarianism. I'm against the scientists and other 'wise' men who rail against God; the likes of Francis Crick, Richard Dawkins, Stephen Hawking, Yuval Harari, and the like.

In most instances, the data collected by the historical geologists is not contentious. What is contentious is the interpretations they've put on that data. Unfortunately, the data on which historical geology is based has been almost entirely paleontological; and the perspective from which that data has been interpreted has, without any justifiable basis, been that of uniformity and spontaneous origin and the spontaneous, non-divine biological evolution of man.

It's reassuring to be able to say that many geologists are critical of uniformitarianism. For example, Doctor Robin S. Allen (*Geological Correlation*

& Paleoecology, *Bulletin of the Geological Society of America*, Vol 59, January 1949) referred to "…the present deplorable state our discipline, a pseudo-science composed (as has been pointed out by other geologists such as R.H. Rastall and Edmund M. Spieker) as being a patchwork of circular reasoning, speculation, dogmatic uniformitarianism and procrustean interpretations – a system purporting to expound the entire evolutionary history of the earth and its inhabitants, yet all the while filled with enumerable gaps and contradictions."

These gaps and contradictions are gaping. Yet even many professing Christians have sought to harmonise uniformist historical geology with Christianity. As this chapter will show, that is an impossibility. If you accept uniformitarianism then, by definition, you are guided by your ego intellect and you have renounced Christian scripture (you have renounced God and Christ); there's no middle ground.

It's a case of scriptural testimony verses an ego-driven philosophy of invented historical geology and the invented spontaneous, non-divine origin and biological evolution of man. It's not a stand-off between scriptural testimony and legitimate or justifiable scientific standpoints. It's a case of scriptural truth versus scientific untruth.

Uniformitarianism, like the theory of Darwinian spontaneous, non-divine origin and biological evolution of man, is nothing more than ego-driven humanist propaganda.

The Scriptural Creation… And God-Caused Catastrophes…

To those who accept the Christian scripture as a true witness of what has been and what is to come events such as the Genesis Flood of Noah's day are historical fact; and they won't be swayed by the scientific arguments of man's ego intellect to the contrary.

Some professing Christians have surrendered to arguments that deny the Genesis Flood and yet believe that they are true Christians. They're not. They're in a no-man's land. Their ego has betrayed them.

Uniformitarianism is not totally invalid or false. When it comes to the state of the Earth the concept is not at odds with scripture. Genesis 8:22 makes it clear that there is and will be an underlying pattern or stability in how the Earth operates. In other words, there is a predictability; and that's because the Creator has said that it will be so.

However, God owns the creation and has clearly stated that the creation itself groans under the weight of man's wrongdoing or 'lawlessness' (Romans 8:21-22); which is why He has used the creation, events such as the Great Flood, to warn mankind. However, uniformitarianism does not recognise as real these divine events (the scriptural doctrine of 'catastrophism'), so, scientists generally deny them, and say that those who believe in them are to be pitied.

Some people, even professing Christians, cannot bear to be thought of or labelled as moronic so they succumb to this bullying. By doing so they fail the test of faith that God has set for each of us, including these idiotic believers in man's spontaneous, non-divine biological origin and evolution.

Insight: According to scholarly research the Great Flood is believed to have occurred in 2304 BC, give or take 11 years: Dr John Osgood, *Creation 4*, 10 to 12 March 1981. This would put the Fall of Adam and Eve at, say, 3960 BC; or 5980 years ago, as at 2020.

The Genesis Flood (The Book)...

This book is the result of painstaking investigation and analysis. What the authors have concluded is set out below.

First, the Great Flood reached its maximum depth after forty days of non-stop torrential rain; the waters did not continue to rise after that; but the entire Earth's surface was submerged for five months before the waters began to fall. The deluge probably lasted 371 days; just over a year before it subsided.

Secondly, Noah's ark was 437.5 feet (133.35 m) long, 72.92 feet (22.22 m) wide and 43.75 feet (13.33 m) high; with three decks with a total deck area of about 95,700 square feet (8,891 m^2) with a total volume of 1,396,000 cubic feet (39,530 cubic metres).

Insight: If the Flood had been only local, rather than universal, not only would an arc of such a size not have been needed, there would have been no need for an ark at all. Everyone would have just walked to higher or drier ground; and, plainly, there would have been no need for Noah to rescue birds of flight unless the flood was, indeed, universal.

Thirdly, the New Testament supports the happening of the Flood and its magnitude. It's referred to in detail in 2 Peter 3:3-7. This scripture is worth reading because in it, Peter warns (prophesies) that "... in the last days..." mockers will come "... walking after their won lusts...".

Peter also warns Christians against believing false teachers [atheist scientists?] and against backsliding (that is, against being bullied or intimidated by the likes of Richard Dawkins) (2 Peter 2:18-22).

Peter warns us all against choosing to believe the teachings of man where they conflict with what God says.

Fourthly, all humans and animals on the Earth that were not rescued by Noah died in the Flood; and Genesis 6 tells us, plainly, that the purpose of the Flood was to wipe out a sinful and degenerate humanity. Again, the New Testament corroborates this account. The apostle Peter tells us that only eight souls were saved (1 Peter 3:20). Remember, God had commanded man to 'fill the Earth' (Genesis 1:28), so all the rest of mankind, world-wide, perished.

Fifthly, there will be similar catastrophes at the time of Christ's second coming (Luke 17:26-30); Matthew 24:39). However, God has promised that this time not all of humanity and not every living will be destroyed (Genesis 8:21; 9:11-15).

Sixthly, it's conservatively estimated that there were, say, 18 generations (with an average life-span of, say, 90 years in the estimated 1656 years from Adam to the Flood). This equates, conservatively, to a world population of about 774 million as at the time of the Flood. This would be about the population of the Earth in say the late nineteenth century.

I don't intend to delve further into *The Genesis Flood* as it's something the serious reader can do.

What You Have Learned in This Chapter

- Man's ego, especially his intellectual ego, doesn't want to let a divine foot in the door because man's ego wants to be 'god'.
- As back-stop, man's spiritual ego will allow a divine foot in the door but it will re-interpret the scripture to make a god of its liking rather than God
- As long as you allow your intellectual or spiritual egos to shape your beliefs you are lost
- Truth and freedom require that you cast off your ego, that you practice humility and that's something few can do

- It takes enormous courage to gainsay the politically correct view that the theory of man's spontaneous, non-divine biological origin and evolution is sacrosanct, but it's a miniscule price to pay in the long run

Chapter 16

David Hawkins' Flawed Views on the Christian Scripture and on God...

What You'll Discover in This Chapter...

- David Hawkins believed in 'God' but didn't 'know' the God of the Christian scripture
- His view that most of the Old Testament and the New Testament Book of Revelation of the New Testament, are 'false', is flawed
- He appeared to believe, at least to a degree, that there is mortal reincarnation, but according to Christian scripture there is no such thing
- He appears not to have had Christian faith, although he may have had faith based on a syncretised (that is, a blended) belief system
- Even high consciousness, as measured on Hawkins' MoC, is not on the same level as Christian faith in God

David Hawkins Wrote About Man... And God...

It seems that David Hawkins realised there is a Creator God; which explains why the dedication in his books is 'Gloria in Excelsis Deo!' (meaning 'Glory to God in the Highest!'); taken from the Christian hymn written by Johann Sebastian Bach in Leipzig, Saxony, in about 1745. The hymn is based on Luke Chapter 2 which recounts the birth of Jesus, the Christ (the Messiah).

Hawkins Denies the Veracity of Much of the Christian Scripture...

In his book *Truth vs Falsehood* (p388), in the table that refers to the prophesied end times, Hawkins says that these prophesies calibrate as false using the kinesiological muscle test. In his book *Reality, Spirituality, and Modern Man* (pp117 and 241) he says, in effect, that the Book of Revelation in the New Testament is also false. He seems to have considered only Genesis and Psalms of the Old Testament to be valid (*Reality, Spirituality, and Modern Man*, p193).

Paradoxically, Hawkins said in *Power vs Force* (p388):

"Destiny is determined by the level of consciousness and choices thereby available, plus unknown factors, such as Grace, Salvation, Divine Mercy and Intercessors via faith and worship. The karma of atheism, as hatred of God, or denunciation of Divinity itself, all calibrate at very serious levels of 40-70, thus indicating a very dire spiritual destiny... In contrast, atheism as an intellectual/philosophical position calibrates at 165-190, which is the level of (intellectual) pride."

This is a paradoxical stance for Hawkins to have taken, because, by recognising a divine God, Hawkins implicitly recognised Jesus (God of the Son, part of Elohim) as being Divine as well as mortal; yet he, in effect, denies Jesus by his denials of part of the Christian scripture; as I will seek to show.

The Main Books of Prophecy from the Christian Scripture...

About 25% to 28%, or thereabouts, of the Christian scripture is prophecy (history told in advance). The rest tells us about creation, including our creation, truth, the presence of untruth, God's plan for mankind, how we will, by our choices in life, choose our own destiny, the 'good news' (gospel) and God's master plan for the salvation of the righteous.

Insight: 'Righteous' does not mean 'sinless'.

Prophecy is unique to Christian scripture; and is extraordinary because it has been thoroughly tested, scientifically, and been shown to be 'true', refer to Professor Stoner's work, detailed in Chapter 13 of this book.

The main book of prophecy of the Old Testament is Daniel; but there is prophecy in many other Old Testament books; such as Isaiah, Jeremiah, Ezekiel, Lamentations, Micah, Habakkuk, Psalms, and so on.

The major prophecies of the New Testament are found in the Olivet Prophecy of Jesus (Matthew 24 and 25, Mark 13 and Luke 21); sometimes called the prophecy of the 'Little Apocalypse', because it seems to pre-empt, at least in part, the prophecies in the second major prophetic book of the Old Testament: The Book of Revelation.

Insight: The Olivet Prophecy came from Jesus, the mortal man. The Book of Revelation was given to the apostle John by the risen Jesus Christ. That is, both are prophecies directly from Jesus the man and Jesus Son of God (part of the Elohim).

A Dire Warning from the New Testament Book of Revelation...

The Book of Revelation contains a dire warning in the fourth and third last verses of the last chapter (Revelation 22:18-19):

> "(18) For I testify to everyone who hears the words of the prophecy of this book: 'If anyone adds to these things, God will add to him the plagues that are written in this book'.
>
> (19) and if anyone takes away from the words of the book of this prophecy God shall take away his part from the Book of Life, from the holy city, and from the things which are written in this book."

It seems to me that if anyone denies the validity of the Book of Revelation as David Hawkins appears to have done (*Truth vs Falsehood*, p388, in the table that says the Prophesied End Times are 'false', and *Reality, Spirituality, and Modern Man*, pp117-140) is playing with fire.

By denying the Book of Revelation Hawkins also denies the New Testament Olivet Prophesy of Jesus, as I will show.

Some Basics About God, Jesus the Messiah and the Christian Scripture...

First: God is and always has been plural, a duality: God the Father and God the Son. That's why in Genesis 1:26 it reads:

"Then God said, 'Let Us [not *Me*, but *Us*] make man in *Our* image, according to *Our* likeness'..."

The plural name for God the Father and God the Son is 'Elohim', the singular is Eloah, (Hebrew: God). God the Son gave up His divine status to become Jesus and then returned to be God the Son after His crucifixion.

Although God is plural (Elohim) Jesus and God the Father are 'One' (John 10:30). He who has seen Jesus (God the Son) has seen God the Father (John 14:7-9), because they are One.

Second: Jesus knew of His former divine status: "Truly, truly, I say to you before Abraham was born, I AM" (John 8:58). He was on a different level and of a different status than, say, Buddha; who was a mere mortal like the rest of us. There is no comparison between the two.

The coming of Jesus and His status were foretold by other prophets, such as Moses. Jesus said that Moses wrote about Him (John 5:46-47); and Jesus was acknowledged by others, while in His mortal state, as being sent by God.

John the Baptist acknowledged Jesus as *the Lamb of God who takes away the sin of the world* (John 1:29). It was John the Baptist who opened the way for Jesus to receive the Holy Spirit from God the Father, by baptising Him (Matthew 3). God had told us long before the time of John the Baptist, that He would send Jesus to give us a path to eternal life (Isaiah 52:13).

It was following the baptism of Jesus that we are told: "And after He was baptised Jesus came up immediately out of the water, and behold, the heavens were open to Him and He saw the Spirit of God descending as a dove, and coming upon Him. And lo, a voice from Heaven said, 'This is My beloved son in whom I am well pleased'." (Matthew 3:16-17). However, like John the Baptist (Luke 1:15) it seems that Jesus may have already had the Holy Spirit within Him in the womb, but this is not clear from the scripture. We do know that Jesus did not come to Earth in His divine glory (Philippians 2:5-8) and He did not come knowing everything (Matthew 24:36; Luke 2:40 and 5:17).

In other words, what finished the preparation of Jesus as a mortal, to befit Him for His mortal ministry (following His baptism), was the intervention of God the Father, who implanted the Holy Spirit within Him.

Third: the tearing of the Temple Veil in Jerusalem at the moment of Jesus' death by Crucifixion is part of the story of Jesus' role on Earth, and part of your story and mine. The tearing of the temple veil is recorded in Matthew 27:51 and Mark 15:38; as is the fact that He died at the precise moment of the sacrifice for Passover was held.

In Exodus 26:31-35, Moses was given instructions regarding the Temple Veil. It was to be woven of blue, purple and scarlet thread (which is the source of the colours of the Israelites: red, white and blue) hung on four pillars of acacia wood overlaid with gold. The hooks were to be made of gold, upon four sockets of silver.

The temple was the place where animal sacrifices were performed. The temple veil separated the Holy of Holies from the rest of the temple, where the worshippers could congregate (Hebrews 9:1-9). The veil signified that man was separated from God by sin (Isaiah 59:1-2).

Only the High Priest was permitted to pass beyond this veil, once each year (Exodus 30:10; Hebrews 9:7), to enter into God's presence, in the Holy of Holies, for all of Israel, to make atonement for their sins (Leviticus 16).

It's estimated that the temple veil was about 60 feet high. It was deliberately made to be thick and strong.

Nonetheless, at the moment of Jesus' death the temple veil was torn in two, from top to bottom (Matthew 27:50-51). This symbolised that the animal sacrifices were now redundant having been replaced by the sacrifice of Jesus; that henceforth, the only means of atonement for man's sins was through Jesus; and only through Jesus; that each person, Jew and Gentile, had access to God, through the sacrifice of Jesus provided they became and remain 'righteous'. No other person in history, including Buddha and all the great sages, has had such a status or role.

Insight: 'Righteous' does not mean 'sinless'. 'Righteous' also does not mean you have attained a particular LoC on David Hawkins' MoC.

Fourth: God has always had a plan for mankind; and His plan will be fulfilled no matter what; but most of humanity will not have a role in God's plan because they will have squandered their chance for God's grace and resurrection into His Kingdom by the poor choices they make; such as the choice not to acknowledge God, the gospel and the sacrifice Jesus and a failure to choose righteousness as their way of life.

In brief, God's plan has been to expand the God family. Those admitted to membership will be those who are given God's grace and resurrection into His kingdom; the righteous. Plainly, it will not include non-believers, or those who merely masquerade as believers, or those who merely pay slip-service to God and the scripture, or those who have syncretised belief systems; that is, ego-tainted beliefs.

Sages are Just Sages...

It isn't clear to me whether David Hawkins drew much of a distinction, in practical terms, between mere sages, such as Buddha, on the one hand, and Jesus, on the other.

I have watched a *YouTube* recording of David Hawkins that I believe was made in about 2002. In that recording he said to the effect that the difference between Buddha and Jesus was that Buddha came to show the way to 'enlightenment' (whatever that means) and Jesus came to provide salvation. That is an ambiguous and incomplete answer so far as Jesus is concerned.

Who Needs Salvation...?

According to David Hawkins, salvation is only necessary for those below LoC 600 on the MoC (*The Eye of the I*, p404). Hawkins appears to be saying that if you get to LoC 600 you don't need Jesus; but he doesn't make clear, what happens after you die and that's a big issue, as I hope I will show. I cannot see how David Hawkins, or sages such as Buddha, could be considered truly conscious if they do not know the purpose of human life.

Why are We Here...?

According to David Hawkins, (*Power vs Force*, p314) the purpose of human life on Earth is 'obscure', but he also said that his research confirmed the divine incarnation of Jesus (*Reality, Spirituality, and Modern Man*, p101).

Jesus and Sages Such as Buddha... Worlds Apart...

Christian scripture stands apart from all other writing in that it contains prophecy (that is, history told in advance). Buddhism, Hinduism, Scientology, Bahai and Rasta and David Hawkins MoC, for example, do not have prophets or prophecy. At best, their spokesmen are sages.

One of the prophets of the Old Testament was Moses who lived about 1500 years before Jesus. I base this calculation on my belief that Moses led the Israelites out of Egypt, on their Exodus, in about 1445 BC (or possibly 40 years earlier); during the reign of Pharaoh Amenhotep (who was Pharaoh from 1447 BC to 1421 BC, following the death of his father Thutmose III).

Amenhotep was succeeded by Thutmose IV who reigned from 1421 BC to 1410 BC. In what appears to be a reference to Amenhotep, the Dream Stela of

Thutmose IV seems to verify that Pharaoh's first-born son died before Pharaoh agreed to let Moses take the Israelites out of Egypt.

Insight: some eminent writers suggest that Moses was born in 1567 BC and died in 1447 BC (aged 120 years); and that the Exodus occurred in 1487 BC, when Thutmose II was the Pharaoh.

Jesus referred to the laws given to Moses (Matthew 5:17; 19:17; 23:2-3; Mark 7:9-10; 10:2-9; 10:18-19; Luke 5:14; 16:29-31; 18:19-20; John 5:45-47). Jesus also said that Moses wrote about Him (John 4:46).

So, already, we see that Jesus was written about more than a thousand years before His birth; but the same cannot be said of Buddha or any of the sages. Sages aren't divine, they're not prophets; and they are not of the same status as Jesus.

Jesus Verified Much of the Old Testament...

By the age of 12, Jesus was already more than a match for the teachers in the Temple (Luke 2:40-50). He confounded the Pharisees when it came to who the son of David is (Matthew 22:41-46).

One of the books of the Old Testament that David Hawkins considered false was Deuteronomy, the book Moses wrote when he was dying. The word 'Deuteronomy' literally means 'these are the words' but is generally understood to mean the 'second statement' of God's law, or reiteration of God's law, by Moses. Jesus, Himself, endorsed Deuteronomy by using passages from the book when resisting the temptations of Satan (Matthew 4:1-11).

The books of the Old Testament that Jesus appears to have quoted most are Exodus, Isaiah, Deuteronomy and Psalms:

Jesus referenced the burning bush	Acts 7:30-34	Exodus 3:1-6
Jesus referred to the Ten Commandments	Mark 10:17-25	Exodus 20:12-16
Jesus mentioned the Fifth Commandment (honouring parents) when showing that the scribes and Pharisees were hypocrites	Matthew 15:14	Exodus 20:12
Jesus quoted the scripture on 'an eye for an eye'	Matthew 5:38-48 Romans 12:17-19	Exodus 21:22-25 Leviticus 24:19-22 Deuteronomy 19:19-21 Proverbs 20:22
Jesus spoke in parables concerning 'eyes that do not see' and 'ears that do not hear'	Mark 8:18	Isaiah 6:9-10 Jeremiah 5:21

185

When Jesus turned over the tables in the temple, He refers to the words of Isaiah on how the house of God should operate	Matthew 21:13 Mark 11:17 Luke 19:46	Isaiah 56:7
Jesus criticised the scribes and Pharisees for paying only lip service to God	Matthew 15:8-9 Mark 7: 6-7	Isaiah 29:13
Jesus alluded to Isaiah in his parable of the vineyard	Matthew 21:33 Mark 21:1 Luke 20:9	Isaiah 5:1
Jesus quoted Isaiah's prophecy that He would die a sinner's death	Luke 22:37	Isaiah 53:12
Jesus summed up the law and the prophets with references to Deuteronomy and Leviticus	Matthew 22:37 Mark 12:29-33 Luke 10:27	Deuteronomy 6:5 Leviticus 19:18
Jesus references Deuteronomy when he talks of divorce	Matthew 5:31; 19:7 Mark 10:4	Deuteronomy 24:1-3
Jesus referred to Moses' rule of witnesses when He spoke of church discipline	Matthew 18:16	Deuteronomy 19:15
Jesus quoted Psalm 22 when dying on the cross: "My God, my God, why have You forsaken Me."	Matthew 27:46 Mark 15:34	Psalm 22:1
Jesus quoted Psalm 31 by committing His spirit to the Father	Luke 23:46	Psalm 31:5
Jesus was hated without cause which He says the Psalms foretold	John 15:25	Psalm 35:19; 69:4
Jesus quoted the Psalms when talking of His betrayal	John 13:18	Psalm 41:9
Jesus quoted Psalm 110 when asked by Pilate whether He was the son of God. Jesus explains Psalm 110:1 in Mark 12:35-37; Luke 20:41	Matthew 26:64	Psalm 110:1
Jesus quoted Psalms to the chief priests and elders when He referred to Himself as the chief cornerstone of the church. Note: This also shows that the claim of the Roman Catholic Church that the apostle Peter was or is the cornerstone of the church (and the first Pope) is false	Matthew 21:42 Mark 12:10 Luke 20:17	Psalm 118:22-23
Jesus referred to Psalms when prophesying the destruction of Jerusalem. Note: Jerusalem was sacked by the Roman General Titus (son of the Roman Emperor Vespasian), in 70 AD. The temple (the 'house' of the priests referred to by Jesus in Luke 13:35) was totally destroyed. Even the stone floors were torn up. The gold taken from the temple was used to fund the construction of the Colosseum in Rome; completed in 79 AD. Jerusalem will be destroyed again before Jesus returns	Matthew 23:19 Luke 13:35 Matthew 24:15	Psalm 118:26

Jesus quoted many more books and prophets of the Old Testament, including Daniel (Matthew 24:15); but the above sampling makes the point. One has to ask: how, then, could David Hawkins possibly question the veracity or legitimacy of any of the scriptures, on the one hand, while, on the other hand, recognising Jesus.

Interviews for Jesus and Buddha...

Let's say we could ask some key questions of Jesus and Buddha, what would they likely say? Let's take a look.

Jesus

1	Question:	Are you a prophet?
	Answer:	Yes; and I am also God the Son, part of the Elohim
2	Question:	Can you tell us what the purpose of earthly life is?
	Answer:	Yes, that's why I'm here; and that's why, by My name 'Logos' or 'Word' I gave the prophets of the Old Testament their prophecies and tasks
3.	Question:	Did you come to offer a path to salvation for mankind?
	Answer:	Yes; and to reveal the gospel (good news)
4.	Question:	Will you intercede for us with God to try to save us?
	Answer:	Yes, that is my role; and I will be the one who judges each person
5	Question:	Would you die for us?
	Answer:	Yes, that's why I came. I am the ultimate sacrifice and the one and only gateway to resurrection
6.	Question:	Will following your path give eternal life?
	Answer:	Yes. You must be baptised by full immersion and be righteous
7.	Question:	Do you provide a means of salvation for us?
	Answer:	Yes, it's through Me; My mortal death. I am the gate to eternal salvation
8	Question:	Is there a Supreme Being?
	Answer:	Yes, God, the Elohim, of which I am part
9	Question:	Have you prophesied our future?
	Answer:	Yes. The prophecies of the Old Testament were inspired by me (God the Son, the Logos, the Word) to the prophets. I gave the Olivet Prophecy to my disciples during my mortal life, shortly before My crucifixion, and I inspired My servant John to record the Book of Revelation after My mortal death

10	Question:	Have you done miracles on Earth?
	Answer:	Yes
11	Question:	Do humans have souls?
	Answer:	Yes, and more importantly, humans have spirit
12	Question:	Can God's Word (the Christian scriptures) be legitimately changed by us, interpreted or given our own spin?
	Answer:	No! I am the Word and the Word is forever

Buddha

1	Question	Are you a prophet?
	Answer:	What's a prophet?
2	Question:	Can you tell us what the purpose of earthly life is?
	Answer:	Pass
3.	Question:	Did you come to save us?
	Answer:	How on Earth could I do that! I'm already dead! Save you from what?
4	Question:	Will you intercede for us with the Supreme Being to try to save us?
	Answer:	Pass. What Supreme Being?
5	Question:	Would you die for us?
	Answer:	No. You have to die for yourself by achieving Nirvana. Good Luck!
6	Question:	Will following your path give eternal life?
	Answer:	No. It will lead you to Nirvana: eternal death
7.	Question:	Do you provide a means of salvation for us?
	Answer:	No. I can't. I'm dead
8.	Question:	Is there a Supreme Being?
	Answer:	Pass
9.	Question:	Have you prophesied our future?
	Answer:	What's prophecy? I don't have a future. I hope you attain Nirvana so that you don't have a future too
10	Question:	Do you do miracles on Earth?
	Answer:	What's a miracle?
11	Question:	Do humans have souls?

	Answer:	Pass
12.	Question:	Can God's word (the Christian scriptures) be legitimately changed by us, interpreted or given our own spin?
	Answer:	I have no idea what you refer to by God's word, or the scripture. What's that about? What does 'Christian' mean?

What if we Looked at the CVs for Moses, Buddha, Confucius and Jesus...

I've included Moses and Confucius because they were mortals, like you and me. I've left out Krishna because although he is said to have been, at some stage, an earthly incarnation of Vishnu (whatever that means) and is said to have lived on Earth in about 300-200 BC, I'm not aware of him delivering prophecy (history told in advance) or claiming to fulfil end-time prophecies. I've included Buddha and Confucius as a means of contrast between perceived wise men; as they were totally different.

Moses

Birth Date: circa 1567 BC
Birth Place: Egypt
Nationality: Israelite (Levite) and Egyptian by adoption
Occupation: Court official in Egypt, Prophet
Date of Death: circa 1447 BC
Cause of Death: God's decree
Age at Death: 120 years
Available to answer prayers: No
Major Roles: Led the Exodus circa 1487-1446 BC of the Israelites from Egypt. Received Gods' revelation to the Israelites, including law.

Buddha

Birth Date: 563 BC
Birth Place: What is now Nepal
Nationality: 'Indian', or Nepalese
Occupation: Philosopher, Sage, (hermit?)
Date of Death: 480 BC

Cause of Death: Not known

Age at Death: 80 years

Available to answer prayers: No

Major Roles: Developed and taught what is now referred to as various styles/types of Buddhism

Confucius

Birth Date: 551 BC

Birth Place: China

Nationality: 'Chinese'

Occupation: Court official in Emperor's service

Date of Death: 478 BC

Cause of Death: Not known

Age at Death: 74 years

Available to answer prayers: No

Major Roles: Developed and taught Confucianism, a code for life

Jesus

Birth Date: 5 BC (between 27 August and 9 September)

Birth Place: Bethlehem, Judea

Nationality: Israelite (Judean)

Occupation: Carpenter

Date of Death: Wednesday, 5 April, 30 AD (the Passover, Nisan 14).

Cause of Death: Execution by Crucifixion

Age at Death: 34 years

Available to answer prayers: Yes

Major Roles: Died to provide a gateway to salvation for humankind; the God of the Old Testament (the Logos, the Word), God the Son (part of Elohim).

Jesus in the Old Testament...

In John 5:39 Jesus said:

"You [referring to the Jews in Jerusalem] search the Scriptures [which at the time meant the Books of the Old Testament, as the New Testament had not been written] for in them you think you have eternal life; and these are they [that is, the Scriptures] which testify of Me."

Plainly, Jesus was saying that there are references to Him in the Books of the Old Testament.

The first reference to the coming of Jesus, the Messiah, Saviour and Redeemer is in Genesis 3:15, where Eve was promised that a male descendent from her line would crush the head of the serpent (that is, Satan).

The name of Jesus in Hebrew is 'Yeshua'. Matthew 1:21 refers to what was well understood by the Jewish people: that the name Yeshua means 'salvation' or 'God saves'. Matthew 1:21 states that the son born of Mary is to be called Jesus, as he will save His people from their sins. In Matthew 1:23 it stated that the people will refer to Jesus as 'Immanuel' meaning 'God with us'. In John 14:9, Jesus said those who have seen Him have seen the Father.

In Matthew 5:18, Jesus made it absolutely clear that every part of the Old Testament stands.

To put matters beyond doubt, about the veracity of the Old Testament, Habakkuk 3:13 virtually gives the name of Jesus, by referring to Him as the saviour and the anointed. In the Hebrew the word 'Yesha' (a variant of Yeshua, meaning Jesus) clearly refers to the Jesus of the New Testament.

This being the case, how can David Hawkins suggest that any of the Books of the Old Testament are false?

Now Let's Also Look at the Old Testament Prophet Daniel... And the New Testament Book of Revelation...

Jesus endorsed what was written by the prophet Daniel in the Old Testament (Matthew 24:15); where Daniel refers to the abomination of desolation, part of the great tribulation that is spoken of in the New Testament Book of Revelation.

Daniel was an Israelite living in the Kingdom of Judah at the time it was conquered by King Nebuchadnezzar of Babylon in 587 BC. He went into captivity in Babylon. Although a captive, Daniel rose to a high position the Babylonian Court; and in the Persian Court after the Persians conquered Babylon. Daniel is famous for having been cast into the lion's den by the Babylonians. Because of his faith in God, he survived.

The Book of Daniel is the final book of the four major prophets of the Old Testament (Isaiah, Jeremiah, Ezekiel and Daniel). His book is divided into two parts. The first part (Chapters 1-6) tells the story of Daniel and his compatriots.

The second part (Chapters 7-12) contains Daniel's visions and prophecies. Daniel foresaw and described:

- The great world empires that were to come
- The coming of Jesus Christ
- The end-times

Probably the most spectacular aspect of Daniel's prophecies is the '70 weeks' prophecy (Daniel 9:24-27) in which he tells us that God has specified a period of 70 'sevens' or '7 weeks of years' to complete the salvation of the Israelites. Daniel correctly foretold that a total of 69 of these 'weeks of years' (that is, 483 years) would elapse from the time that the temple at Jerusalem was ordered to be rebuilt until the Messiah (that is, Jesus) appeared.

Solomon's Temple (the original temple) was built in about 1007 BC (480 years after the Exodus; and was destroyed by the Babylonian King Nebuchadnezzar. Astonishingly, the order to rebuild Solomon's temple was given in 457 BC by Cyrus (and possibly Artaxerxes) the Great of Persia (Daniel 9:24-27; Isaiah 44:26-28; Isaiah 45:1-4, 13; Jeremiah 29:10; 2 Chronicles 36:23; Ezra 1:1-3) and exactly 483 years later Jesus Christ began his ministry in Galilee.

Daniel's prophecy of the rise of five empires is considered to have already been fulfilled in relation to the first four:

- The Babylonian empire
- The Persian (or Medo-Persian) empire
- The Greek or (Greco-Macedonian) empire
- Ancient Rome

The fifth empire predicted by Daniel is believed to be a reference to a re-emergence of the Roman empire in Europe; and possibly the Holy Roman Empire founded under Charlemagne (Karl the Great) in 800 AD, a union between the Roman Catholic Church and that part of Europe led by Charlemagne.

Daniel also prophesied, hundreds of years in advance, wars between political entities called the 'King of the South' and the 'King of the North'. Historically, these are references to the Ptolomeic Dynasty of Egypt (King of the South) and the King's ruling from Antioch in Syria (King of the North).

The New Testament Olivet Prophecy of Jesus...

I have already noted that the prophesied end-times will last seven years. The first 3.5 years of the end-time events is referred to as the *Tribulation*. The second 3.5 years is referred to as the *Abomination*. The return of Christ is referred to as the *Consummation*.

The Olivet Prophecy (by Jesus as a mortal man) relates to the end-times. It is so called because it refers to prophecy given by Jesus privately to His disciples on the Mount of Olives just a few days before His crucifixion. The Olivet Prophecy is recorded in Matthew 24, Mark 13 and Luke 21 (that is, in the New Testament). The Seven Seals spoken of in the Book of Revelation parallel the Olivet Prophecy.

In the Book of Revelation, the last book of the New Testament, we are told that the 'end times' will last 7 years; of which the first 3.5 years are referred to as tribulation and the second 3.5 years as the 'Abomination'. The point at which Christ returns to Earth (the Second Coming) is referred to as the 'Consummation'.

A Brief Look at The Power of Christian Scriptural Prophecy...

The prophecies of the Christian scripture are compelling because:

- They involve specific places that can be identified even today
- They involve specific people who can be identified even today
- They have been made and recorded as far back as 3,500 years ago
- They fit together
- None of them have failed

God Told Us He Would Give Us Prophecy... And He Has...

In the Book of Isaiah, written about 700-690 BC, God (that is, the God of the Old Testament, the Logos, the Word: the one who became Jesus) told us that He declares to us what will occur beforehand:

"I am the Lord, that is My name; and My glory I will not give to another, nor My praise to carved images. Behold, the former things have come to pass, and new things I declare; before they spring forth I tell you of them" (Isaiah 42:8-9).

"To whom then will you liken Me, or to whom shall I be equal? says the Holy One. Lift up your eyes on high, and see who has created these things, who brings out their host by number; He calls them all by name, by the greatness of His might and by the strength of His power; not one is missing" (Isaiah 40:25-26).

God Challenges Others (Such as Our Scientists and Sages) To State What Will Occur...

"Let them bring forth and show us what will happen; let them show the former things, what they were, that we may consider them, and know the latter end of them; or declare to us things to come. Show the things that are to come hereafter, that we may know that you are gods; yes do good or do evil that we may be dismayed and see it together. Indeed you are nothing, and your work is nothing; he who chooses you is an abomination" (Isaiah 41:22-24).

God Has Stated That He Will Determine What Occurs, No One Else...

"Indeed I have spoken it; I will also bring it to pass. I have purposed it; I will also do it" (Isaiah 46:11).

A few more examples of fulfilled Christian prophecies...

1. Date of Prophecy: Approximately 1400 BC
    Bible Text: Old Testament, Genesis 15:18
    Event: Abraham's descendants will have their own country between the Nile and Euphrates Rivers
    Fulfilled in about 1800 BC. 1400 BC.

2. Date of Prophecy: 701-681 BC
    Bible Text: Old Testament, Isaiah 42:1-9
    Event: The coming of Jesus
    When Fulfilled: Jesus' birth, 5 BC

3. Date of Prophecy: 750-686 BC
    Bible Text: Old Testament, Micah 4:1

Event: Jerusalem's Temple Mount will become the world's most important religious site

When Fulfilled: Site of Solomon's Temple. It is now the site of the Dome of the Rock

4. Date of Prophecy: About 1400 BC
Bible Text: Old Testament, Genesis 49:10
Event: Jesus came from the Israelite tribe of Judah (one of the 12 tribes of Israelites)
When Fulfilled: 5 BC, by Jesus

5. Date of Prophecy: About 750 – 686 BC
Bible Text: Old Testament, Micah 5:2
Event: The Messiah will be born in Bethlehem
When Fulfilled: 5 BC, by Jesus

6. Date of Prophecy: 520 – 518 BC
Bible Text: Old Testament, Zechariah 9:9
Event: The Messiah will enter Jerusalem riding a donkey
When Fulfilled: during Christ's ministry

7. Date of Prophecy: 520 – 518 BC
Bible Text: Old Testament, Zechariah 12:1-5
Event: Jerusalem will become an international issue

When Fulfilled: Since the Balfour Declaration, following World War I. Jerusalem is the only city in the world that is of interest to the rest of the world. In 1947 the UN General Assembly approved a plan to establish Israel.

Date of Prophecy: 30 AD
Bible Text: New Testament, Luke 21:33
Event: Jesus said that His words would never be forgotten regardless of what happens in the world
When Fulfilled: Still being fulfilled

What Is the Gospel...?

The most common and probably most useful explanation is that the term means 'good news'. The fundamental purpose of the scripture is to deliver a good message to humankind.

The gospel comes with warnings that are meant to get our attention and prevent us straying into error.

The first warning is that we have to be careful not to be deceived by false messages (that is, false gospels) or false messengers. The apostle Paul gave this warning (2 Timothy 4:1-4). In 2 Peter 1:20-21 we are cautioned that prophecy (that is, gospel) is not of private interpretation; we are not permitted to twist the words of the gospel.

The second warning springs from the first. We are told that the way to avoid being snared by misrepresentations of the gospel is to test or prove its accuracy and legitimacy (1 Thessalonians 5:21). The only way to do this is to personally read the scriptures, and to do so very carefully. Do not rely on what you are told from the pulpit or what others tell you, including David Hawkins and me. *You must always verify by reference to the scripture.*

We are commanded to study the word (2 Timothy 2:15): "Be diligent to present yourself approved to God, a worker who does not need to be ashamed, rightly dividing the word of truth."

To Assist Us, We are Told: "Do Not Despise Prophecies." (1 Thessalonians 5:20)

This means that the onus is on each of us, as an individual, to verify the gospel for ourselves. We are commanded to do so. We cannot delegate the responsibility to a Church, a Priest, a trusted colleague, David Hawkins, me, or anyone else. The task is yours and mine alone.

The starting point is to understand that "... [the] gospel did not come to you in word only, but also in power and in the Holy Spirit..." (1 Thessalonians 1:5). This is telling us that the gospel is not merely words but also something active that is moving from God. It is not static but dynamic.

The Four Parts of the Gospel...

- The gospel of the Kingdom of God
- The gospel of Grace
- The gospel of Salvation
- The gospel of Peace

I don't share the view of those who say that the gospel is limited to the gospel of the Kingdom of God. These people appear to say that the gospel does not include the sacrifice of Christ and the promise of salvation. In the author's view they are mistaken as soon as they begin to limit the message from God or as soon as they begin to disregard or not include parts of the scripture in the good news message.

How can Jesus be left out of the gospel? How do you even get to the Kingdom of God except through Jesus! The New Testament is about Jesus. If God had wanted to, He could have made the scripture much shorter. He could have made it one-tenth or one-twentieth the size by eliminating huge amounts of information. For example, He could have left out the whole story of Christ: His baptism by John the Baptist, His recruitment of the apostles, His ministry, His crucifixion and His resurrection. But He didn't, because Christ is an integral part of the gospel; and the cornerstone of the Church: The Rock.

A Warning to Those Who Teach False Doctrine...

The scripture tells us that it is extremely important that we do not get the gospel wrong; or, worse still, misrepresent it to others. We are warned that God puts a double curse on those who teach false doctrine (Galatians 1:8-9). We have been given two clear messages:

- Study the word and prove or test the veracity of the gospel by reference to the scripture
- Under no circumstances are we to teach a false gospel or false doctrine

Plainly, we would be preaching a false gospel if we were to limit the extent of the gospel. Therefore, we must be careful not to do this. We have been warned that there will be departures from the true gospel during the end times. This is prophesied (1 Timothy 4:1-5, 16; 2 Timothy 4:1-4).

The gospel of the Kingdom of God is referred to in Mark 1:14-15; 16:15 and Acts 8:12; 20:25; 28:13.

The gospel of the Kingdom of God is telling us about a very real kingdom that will be established on Earth with Christ as the King of Kings and Lord of Lords (Revelation 19:11-16; Revelation 11:15).

When Paul preached of the Kingdom of God he did not do so in isolation. For example, in Acts 28:31 he preaches of the Kingdom of God and the things which concern Christ. This tells us that we cannot contemplate the Kingdom of God without including Jesus Christ.

The gospel of Grace is a gospel about 'unmerited pardon'. We know this because 'grace' means 'unmerited pardon'. That is simple enough. This unmerited pardon does not equate to a licence for humankind to trample over God's Laws, ignoring them as we see fit. This is self-evident because part of the scripture (that is, the gospel) is The Ten Commandments; and we know that Jesus Christ stated clearly that He did not come to do away with God's laws but to fulfil them (Mathew 5:17-19).

The unmerited pardon we are given is a reference to us being forgiven our sins. The mechanism of this forgiveness is the shedding of the blood of Christ; the crucifixion of Jesus. This is an 'unmerited' forgiveness from the penalty of death, because we have not, and cannot, 'earn' it or 'qualify' for it.

This means that we have been given a second chance. It does not mean that we have been let off the hook or that we have been given licence to do as we please.

The fact that grace is part of the gospel is borne out by:

- Acts 11:23, which preaches about Jesus and grace
- Acts 15:11, which preaches salvation through the grace of Christ
- John 1:17, which tells us that the Law was given through Moses but grace and truth came through Jesus Christ
- Romans 3:24, which preaches grace through redemption in Jesus Christ
- Galatians 1:6, which preaches that we were called in the grace of Christ
- Ephesians 1:7, which preaches of redemption through Christ's blood
- Titus 2:11, which preaches about the grace of God that permits salvation which is in Christ Jesus with eternal glory

The gospel of Salvation is something we are told not to neglect (Hebrews 2:1-3). We are also told that there can be no salvation other than through Jesus Christ (Acts 4:10-12). There are many other references in the scripture to this Gospel of Salvation:

- Ephesians 1:1-14 tells us about the riches of Christ's grace and "...the gospel of your salvation..."
- 1 Corinthians 15:1-4 tells us, through the apostle Paul, of the gospel of Christ's death for our sins (v.13)
- 1 John 5:11-13 preaches of eternal life given by Christ
- Psalm 3:8 tells us that salvation belongs to the Lord. If it belongs to Him it has come from Him. As it is 'good news' that has come from Him then, plainly, it is part of the gospel
- Isaiah 45:17 preaches the saving of Israel by the Lord with everlasting salvation
- 1 Chronicles 16:23 (written between 424 and 400 BC) proclaims the 'good news' of salvation
- Zechariah 9:9 (written about 520-475 BC) prophesied "... your King is coming to you; He is just and having salvation, lowly and riding on a donkey..."

This was clear prophecy (good news message) about the coming of Jesus Christ to bring salvation

Acts 4:12 tells us "Nor is there salvation in any other, for there is no other name under Heaven given among men by which we must be saved".

Plainly the rest of the scripture (that is, the rest of the gospel) is meaningless without the gospel of Salvation.

If we leave out salvation, the rest becomes meaningless; because the whole purpose of the gospel is that it is good news *to* and *for humankind*

The gospel of Peace is a significant part of the gospel. Without peace there would appear to be no purpose in there being the Kingdom of God. This is why we are told that Jesus will return to Earth as the Prince of Peace (Isaiah 9:12). Ephesians 6:15 preaches "... the gospel of peace..."

The Kinesiological Muscle Test Doesn't Work on Scripture…

According to David Hawkins (*Power vs Force*, p325) the kinesiological muscle test cannot be used to foretell the future.

That being the case, one has to ask how it could be used to test prophecy in the Old Testament or the New Testament; bearing in mind that the events prophesied had not occurred at the time the prophecies were recorded; and some of the prophecies are fulfilled or to be fulfilled twice! Therefore, to try to test the legitimacy of any scripture containing prophecy cannot work by David Hawkins' own admission. Given that about 25% to 28% of the scripture is prophecy then one wonders how the kinesiological muscle test could ever be used.

Furthermore, I have stated that in my view the MoC derived by David Hawkins is merely the first (and the lowest) tier of a *spiral* of consciousness, that goes to infinity.

Given that Hawkins concedes that Jesus was at the top of his MoC (and I would say that Jesus was far beyond the LoC of 50,000 that Hawkins attributed to archangels: *Truth v Falsehood*, p383) and the scriptures are divinely inspired (that is, emanate from a consciousness far beyond the upper level of Hawkins' MoC) it is inconceivable that the kinesiological muscle test of a mere human could be used to test the scripture, to test such high levels of consciousness.

Let's face it, we are talking about a kinesiological muscle test employed by using the muscles of humans; and humans are not divine and humans are tainted by sin. Therefore, how could the earthly vehicle of human muscle tissue (tainted as it is by sin) ever be used to 'test' the veracity or legitimacy of anything divine?

Insight: Go back and re-read Isaiah 40:25-26 and 42:8-9. And then re-read them, again and again, until it sinks in.

Reincarnation…?

It's not clear to me whether David Hawkins believed that humans are, or can be, reincarnated as humans. In *Truth vs Falsehood* (p387) he says that reincarnation, which he describes as a "… spiritual concept…" calibrates as true; but this is an ambiguous statement because he doesn't explain what he means by the term 'spiritual concept'.

In *Reality, Spirituality, and Modern Man* (pp444-445) however, Hawkins seems to suggest that when we die there is no further mortal life; that is, no reincarnation. In the same book (p324) he refers to each of us having an eternal soul but he doesn't tell us what he means by 'soul'.

I find his position bewildering because in *Power vs Force* (pp243-244) he says:

"Does all of this mean that if we learn to operate on the level of unconditional love, we will become immortal? No. The protoplasm of the physical body is vulnerable to its own genetic programming, as well as to its external environment. But from the view point of consciousness level 500 and above, it appears that death itself is only an illusion, and that life goes on unimpeded by the limitation of perception which results from being localised in a physical body. Consciousness is the vital energy that both gives life to the body and survives beyond the body in a different realm of existence."

To be quite honest, I have no idea what Hawkins' final position is on human reincarnation.

What Does the Scripture Say About Reincarnation...?

Life on this earth is fleeting. You'll not get a second chance at this life. You will not be reincarnated. This is made clear in the Old Testament: Ecclesiastes 9:5-10. Those verses make clear that the living will die. It cautions us to use our time wisely and take full advantage and benefit from the opportunities that we are given.

When you die, you don't go straight to Heaven, or to Hell. You are completely dead (Ecclesiastes 9:5-6) but this death is not the end. In 1 Thessalonians 4:15-17, the apostle Paul refers to our physical death as us having fallen asleep until the coming of the Lord.

Revelation 20:5-6 tells us that there will be a resurrection of judgment (for those who do not know Christ) that will take place after the 1,000-year reign of Jesus Christ: the White Throne Judgment. Those who do know Christ are judged earlier, at the seat of Christ.

We are made mortal and as mortals will die only once (that is, there's no reincarnation: Hebrews 9:27). If you are given eternal life, it does not mean that you are reincarnated, again and again, as a human being. Eternal life is spiritual life that does not end; so it does not involve reincarnation.

It's clear from Hebrews 9:27 that all humans will die once and sometime after this will come judgment. Any of us who are found worthy of eternal life will be restored to life; but that is a resurrection, not reincarnation: John 5:28-29.

What You Have Learned in This Chapter

- It is probable that Hawkins discovered only what is the first, and lowest, tier of what is, in reality, a *spiral* of consciousness rather than a 'map' or chart
- There are many things beyond the upper level (LoC 1000) of consciousness on Hawkins' MoC that are incapable of measurement from this first tier
- It is highly questionable whether the kinesiological muscle test – relying as it does on the physical anatomy of a lowly mortal human – could ever be used to test anything that is beyond the physical world, particularly things that are 'spiritual' (in the Christian scriptural context) – except to the extent that those spiritual things are the creation of men's intellects
- It is inconceivable to think that the MoC can be used to test the Divine, to test God's Word
- David Hawkins' MoC cannot be used to test the legitimacy of the Christian scripture
- Reincarnation is a myth

Chapter 17

A Summary of How to Calibrate David Hawkins' LoCs... and Its Limitations...

What You'll Discover in This Chapter...

- We'll look at the steps David Hawkins discusses in his books about calibrating the LoCs
- We'll find out what pre-conditions are essential for the tests to work
- We'll look at what factors would make the results unreliable
- We'll look at its limitations, flaws and anomalies

Recapping What the MoC and the LoCs Are... Hawkins' Core Premise...

In *Power vs Force* (pp xxvii-xxix) Hawkins says:

"We have at our fingertips a means of accurately distinguishing truth from falsehood, workable from unworkable, benevolent from malign. We can illuminate the hidden forces, hitherto overlooked, that determine human behaviour. We have at our disposal a means of finding answers to previously unresolved personal and social problems. Falsehood need no longer hold sway over our lives."

"This book makes a huge promise, perhaps the biggest promise that has ever been made to you. It can provide you the means by which you may detect if you are being misled."

... "The work presented by this book began in January, 1965, and was finally finished in June, 1994."

"The findings reported in the study were independently derived by the use of the research tool elucidated herein, the kinesiologic response."

The MoC Emerges...

The result of the research by David Hawkins and his team was the creation of the Map of Consciousness (MoC) with the logarithmic calibrations (LoCs) depicting the varying grades of what he refers to as 'consciousness', up to LoC 1000.

I have already stated, in this book, that, in my belief, a more accurate depiction of the MoC would be to show it as an ascending spiral, rather than a table. On this spiral I would depict Hawkins' MoC as the first tier (of many tiers) of the spiral; but that's a matter for another book.

The MoC and the Ego...

In this book, I have identified a way of looking at the ego that enables you to work with it and escape its disastrous gravitational pull. I've referred to the ProtoEgo (that is, the survival ego), to the intellectual ego and to the religious ego.

I've sought to show how these manifestations of ego are obstacles to clarity and truth. In that sense, my ego model could be seen as a practical, and perhaps necessary, counterpart to the MoC; particularly when used in conjunction with the concepts of Spiral Dynamics; but my ego story goes far beyond the bounds of the MoC.

What the Hawkins' Kinesiological Test Is...

The purpose of this chapter is to show how, in his books, David Hawkins described how his kinesiological research tool should be used and then to look at what its limitations are.

Firstly, it's a muscle response tool that operates through your biology, your physiology. In other words, it's not a test that's extrinsic to your anatomy. It doesn't engage your 'spirit'.

Given it's a test that's intrinsic to your anatomical biology, it differs from, say, x-ray, MRI and fMRI.

Hawkins' kinesiological method doesn't involve an 'invasion' of your body. It doesn't introduce something into your body that doesn't belong there (such as chemicals, x-rays or other foreign material). It's a case of your body being asked questions; and it's implied that this occurs with no input by your ego.

What Hawkins Said Kinesiology can do...

As Dr Hawkins explains in *Power vs Force* (pp xxi – xxv):

"Kinesiology is now a well-established science, based on testing of an all-or-none muscle response to stimuli. Positive stimulus provokes a strong muscle response; a negative stimulus results in a demonstrable weakening of the test muscle. Clinical kinesiologic muscle testing has found widespread verification over the last twenty-five years"

"... this kinesiologic response reflects the capacity of the human organism to differentiate not only positive from negative stimuli, but also anabolic (life-enhancing) from catabolic (life-consuming), and, most dramatically, true from false."

"... A positive muscle reaction occurs in response to a statement that is objectively true; a negative response occurs if the test subject is presented with a false statement. This phenomenon occurs independently of the test subject's own opinion or knowledge of the topic, and the response has proven cross-culturally valid in many populations and consistent through time. The test results thus fulfil the scientific requirement of replication and, therefore, reliable verification by other investigators."

"... Moreover, we found that this testable phenomenon can be used to calibrate human levels of consciousness so that an arbitrary logarithmic scale of whole numbers emerges, stratifying the relative power of levels of consciousness in all areas of human experience."

"... In attempting to emphasise the value of this technique as a research tool, examples have been given of its potential uses in a wide range of human activities: speculatively, in art, history, commerce, politics, medicine, sociology, and the natural sciences; pragmatically, in marketing, advertising, research and development; and empirically, in psychological, philosophic, and spiritual-religious inquiry."

"... the results described here are the product of twenty years of investigation and millions of calibrations on thousands of subjects by teams of investigators,..."

"... Despite our mistrust of simplification, we may see two general classes of people in the world: believers and nonbelievers. To the nonbelievers, everything is false until proven true; to the believers, everything said in good faith is probably true unless it is proven false. The pessimistic position of cynical scepticism stems from fear. The more optimistic manner of accepting information arises from self-confidence. Either style works and each has its pros and cons."

The Basic Test Steps...

It takes two people to perform Hawkins' kinesiological test, both of whom must according to Hawkins, be open-minded and unbiased; which immediately tells us that this test is not independent of ego. Cynics will test below LoC 200 and therefore cannot be used for such a test. Cynicism is a factor of intellectual, religious or other manifestations of ego.

The recommended test procedure is as follows:

- Have the subject stand erect, right (or left) arm relaxed at his side, left (or right) arm held out parallel to the floor, elbow straight
- The tester faces the subject and places his left hand on the subject's right shoulder to steady him. Tester then places his right hand on the subject's extended right arm just above the wrist
- Tester tells the subject that he is going to try to push the subject's right arm down as the subject resists with all his strength
- Then the tester pushes down on the subject's right arm fairly quickly, firmly and evenly. The idea is to push just hard enough to test the spring and bounce in the arm, but not so hard that the subject's muscles become fatigued. It's not a question of who is stronger, but of whether the subject's muscle can 'lock' the subject's right shoulder joint against the push. The tester says 'resist' the moment before pressing downwards

The Limitations Flaws and Anomalies in the MoC...

First, Hawkins states that for people to use the kinesiological test both the subject and the tester must be at (and preferably well above) LoC 200 on his MoC.

We now know that his MoC is based on consciousness that leads to 'enlightenment' (whatever that is) and that whatever level of consciousness Hawkins had it did not even lead him to understand the purpose of life. To him it remained 'obscure'. This tells me that Hawkins did not get around to making even the most basic of enquiries; by, for example, studying the Christian scripture.

Secondly, there are glaring omissions from the MoC. For example, at none of the LoCs do we see reference to such things as humility, salvation (notwithstanding that Hawkins believed that Jesus was 'divine' (*Reality, Spirituality and Modern Man*, p101) and that He came to offer salvation (a 'YouTube' video made by David Hawkins in about 2002, in which he said, to the effect, that the difference between Buddha and Jesus was that Buddha came to show the way to 'enlightenment' and Jesus came to provide 'salvation').

However, salvation, like humility, repentance and faith, also do not appear on the MoC.

Thirdly, Hawkins couldn't seem to make his mind up whether or not there is reincarnation; which is plainly an entirely different matter than salvation. I discussed this in some detail in Chapter 16.

Fourthly, Hawkins said that the kinesiological test cannot be used to look forwards. That being the case, how could it possibly be used to test the prophecy in the Old Testament or the New Testament?

Fifthly, Hawkins accepted the divine status of Jesus, which should have meant that he accepted whatever Jesus taught. Jesus, Himself, verified the Old Testament. Indeed, Jesus was the God of the Old Testament.

What You Have Learned in This Chapter...

- The MoC isn't a map that can lead you out of your ego quagmire
- The MoC is misleading and erroneous when it comes to truly spiritual matters as opposed to intellectual ego or spiritual ego 'enlightenment' or philosophy
- Hawkins was plainly mistaken in thinking his MoC or his theories could test the validity of Christian scripture
- The MoC, when it ventures into the spiritual is just another false 'religion' invented by man's intellectual ego or spiritual ego

Chapter 18

It's Your Move... Today and Tomorrow...

What You'll Discover in This Chapter...

- You have the time to remain the same which means you also have the time to change
- You've been given valuable information about the meaning and purpose you can give to your life
- You, and only you, can choose to give your life spiritual meaning

Power Beats Force... But Other Stuff Beats Even Power...

According to David Hawkins you can use either power (the attributes from LoC 200 and above on his MoC) or force (the attributes below LoC 200 on his MoC) to try to make your way in this world; but he didn't mention, and probably didn't realise, that there are things even greater than power that don't register on his MoC.

First, there's spiritual faith in the infinite consciousness, truth and ability of the Creator that David Hawkins realised exists but didn't know. I know David Hawkins did not know God because he didn't know the purpose of human life, including his own. He said that the purpose of life is 'obscure' (*Power vs Force*, p314).

Hawkins also was of the belief that not everyone requires salvation. He expressed the belief that if you have a LoC of 600 or more on his MoC then you don't need salvation (*The Eye of the I*, p404).

Secondly, in addition to spiritual faith is spiritual grace; which refers to the unmerited pardon that will be freely given to righteous believers. They will also receive spiritual rewards commensurate with the good works they do in righteousness. This grace, like salvation, is also beyond the realm of David Hawkins' MoC.

Consciousness... And Attitudes...

It was insightful of David Hawkins to realise that low mind consciousness (which relies on force) and higher mind consciousness (from LoC 200 and above on his MoC) that incorporates power are expressed in completely different attitudes. For example, the various LoCs on his MoC have corresponding attitudes, as this extract from his MoC shows:

LoC	Life View	Level	Emotion	Process
500	Benign	Love	Reverence	Revelation
400	Meaningful	Reason	Understanding	Abstraction
350	Harmonious	Acceptance	Forgiveness	Transcendence
310	Hopeful	Willingness	Optimism	Intention
250	Satisfactory	Neutrality	Trust	Release
200	Feasible	Courage	Affirmation	Empowerment
175	Demanding	Pride	Scorn	Inflation
150	Antagonistic	Anger	Hate	Aggression
125	Disappointing	Desire	Craving	Enslavement
100	Frightening	Fear	Anxiety	Withdrawal
75	Tragic	Grief	Regret	Despondency
50	Hopeless	Apathy	Despair	Abdication
30	Evil	Guilt	Blame	Destruction
20	Miserable	Shame	Humiliation	Elimination

Heart... And Attitude...

But what if we were to prepare a list of attitudes that are necessary to go beyond this realm of consciousness to a realm where we can make true enquiry (that is, not merely intellectual enquiry) about who and what you are; about, say the purpose of human life, which David Hawkins did not discern and which does not register on his MoC. It might look like this:

- Humility
- The courage to find the truth
- Intention to find the truth
- Trust (faith without proof) and an honest, open, enquiring heart

"Blessed are the pure in heart, for they will see God" (Matthew 5:8)
"Trust in the Lord with all your heart and lean not on your own understanding" (Proverbs 3:5)

- optimism

It's a Matter of Heart... Not Mind... Not Intellect...

It's a simple yet compelling fact that the scripture talks a great deal about our hearts; rather than our intellect, intelligence, qualifications or achievements.

"Above all else guard your heart, for everything you do flows from it" (Proverbs 4:23).

"I will give them a heart to know Me, that I am the Lord. They will be My people and I will be their God, for they will return to Me with all their heart" (Jeremiah 24:7, NIV).

The whole message of the Christian scripture, from the time of the Old Testament, has been God's plan to transform all people to be like Him, starting with their hearts. This message continues through the New Testament (Matthew 16:18). In other words, you cannot impress God by having a high IQ, by being intellectually gifted, or by great intellectual works. God looks firstly and foremostly at your heart.

God summarised what He intended to accomplish through Jesus Christ:

"I will make an everlasting covenant with them, that I will not turn away from doing them good; but I will put My fear in their hearts so that they will not depart from Me" (Jeremiah 32:40).

It is plain that before the time of Jesus people had generally not been transformed in their hearts. Moses told his people:

"The Lord has not given you a heart to perceive and eyes to see and ears to hear" (Deuteronomy 29:4).

Only a few of the people before the time of Jesus, such as the prophets, had righteous hearts.

The Heart Thinks...

David Hawkins' MoC perhaps gives the impression that we think with our minds, and only with our minds; but he did say (*Power vs Force*, p176) that whereas the intellect is easily fooled the heart recognises the truth.

Whether knowingly or not, Hawkins appears to have been paraphrasing the Old Testament, Proverbs 3:5:

"Trust in the Lord with all your heart and lean not on your own understanding."

Proverbs 2:10 (Old Testament) tells us to the effect that spiritual wisdom enters the heart rather than the mind. In other words, we 'know' with our heart when we allow our heart to be guided by God.

The heart thinks (New Testament, Matthew 9:4; Mark 2:8), remembers, reflects and meditates (Psalm 77:5-6; Luke 2:19).

We are also told that our heart acts as our true conscience (Old Testament, 1 Samuel 24:5; New Testament, Acts 2:37). David prayed to God to create for him a pure heart to replace his defiled conscience (Psalm 51:10).

The heart is where we plan, make commitments – and even decisions (Old Testament, Proverbs 16:9) because our egos can penetrate our hearts; and an ego-driven heart can devise wicked schemes. God hates the things of the ego: pride, lies, evil hands, evil thoughts and those who sow discord (Old Testament Proverbs 6:16-19).

Insight: Plainly, God hates the fruits of selfish, unbridled ego, because the ego has a disobedient, unrighteous proclivity.

David Hawkins' MoC and Love...

Hawkins saw love as a level of consciousness. Love appears at LoC 500 on his MoC. He said that at LoC 540 it became unconditional love (*Truth v Falsehood*, p53). In fact, ego-less love – the love where one does not ask for anything in return – is beyond the mind and beyond consciousness. It belongs to a level of awareness that is beyond Hawkins' MoC; because it's based not merely on so-called 'enlightenment' but on knowing the meaning and purpose of one's life and the lives of others. This is why the greatest example of love is spoken of in 1 John 4:10; where we are told that God so loved us that He sent His son to be the propitiation for our sins (that is, for our wanton ego-driven behaviour).

'The Fall' And Sin...

To my mind, David Hawkins did not understand what the Fall of Adam and Eve was about, or what sin is; notwithstanding that he wrote about them. I can see he instinctively knew that the Fall and sin are central to who and what we currently are, and what we need to escape from; but he didn't know how or why. I could write a great deal about this; but I don't want to take my readers too far with that topic in this book, which is, after all, about the human ego.

Insight: I would say that the Fall was the beginning of the human ego's manifestation as an anthropocentric entity; when we (Adam and Eve) decided that man knew better than God what we are about. It's been a disastrous journey since then, because we've been substituting our plans for us for God's plans for us; and that hasn't worked.

According to David Hawkins (*Reality, Spirituality, and Modern Man*, p34) the Old Testament Book of Genesis (which he said calibrates on his MoC as truthful: *Reality, Spirituality, and Modern Man*, p193) enunciates mankind's collective spiritual inheritance (what he refers to as 'karma') and destiny as a result of:

"... the lapse from the primordial, nonlinear, heavenly paradise (the Garden of Eden) to the descent into proclivity for falsity consequent to falling into the consciousness realm of duality and the linear domain (the dichotomy of good and evil)."

I don't understand why Hawkins didn't just study the scripture to arrive at the truth about what the Fall was, and still is, instead of rationalising it and syncretising it to fit his own world view and his own spiritual view.

What the Fall and Original Sin are Really About...

The Fall is about original sin. So, what does that mean, and are you and I wrongly paying for it? Let's find out with a short and simple explanation of my understanding of original sin.

Insight: Only Adam and Eve are mentioned as being cast out of Eden. There's no mention of them having children before that occurred. We are told, later, that they had children; the first being Cain. He killed his brother Abel. Genesis 4:1 establishes when Cain was conceived and Genesis 3:24 establishes that Adam and Eve had already been expelled from Eden.

Insight: Book 1 of Corinthians, 15:21-22, makes clear that the sinful nature passes from father to child, not from mother to child; which is why Jesus had to be born of a virgin so that He did not have original sin: making Him the second Adam.

Original Sin...

The concept of original sin causes angst for a lot of people. The idea of humankind being born into a condition of sinfulness seems to many to be arbitrary, unreasonable; and, some would say, unjust. Let's see if they're right.

Firstly, let's agree on what we're talking about. The term 'original sin' has two meanings:

- First: it refers to the first sin, committed when Adam and Eve were tempted to eat of the fruit of the tree of the knowledge of good and evil that resulted in 'the Fall'
- Second: it refers to the unrighteous state into which each of the descendants of Adam and Eve have been born as a result of the Fall

The question that then arises is: are we really being punished for what someone else (that is, Adam and Eve) did? Are we in a state of disadvantage vis-à-vis our relationship with our Creator as a result of having been born with the stigma of original sin? If so, why would a just and loving God allow such a thing? In particular, how could God possibly allow 'innocent' babies that die in infancy to be tainted with this sin?

I'll try to answer these questions by giving you my snapshot of how original sin operates. First, we need to understand that there were three significant things in God's sanctuary (the Garden of Eden) at the time of the Fall:

- First: The Tree of Life – that is, the opportunity for eternal life for humankind
- Second: The Tree of the Knowledge of Good and Evil – that is, the capacity for humankind to choose to obey, or (by our ego) to disobey God's laws
- Third: Satan, God's adversary, was there – the one who had attempted to usurp God's power/God's law and replace it with something else

God did not create humankind for His amusement. We are not play-things to Him. He plans to expand His God family by giving the Holy Spirit and eternal life to all of us who are righteous. However, having experienced betrayal by Satan, who, unlike humankind, was created with eternal life, and who also had freedom of choice, God set things up differently for us.

To avoid the possibility of humans choosing to be unrighteous and becoming an eternal problem for Him, God decided that humans must first prove themselves righteous before they can attain eternal life. He therefore decreed that, in the case of humans, they would live, firstly, as mortals so that they would be subject to physical death. We are created so that our physical bodies will die, but the significant death occurs if, following judgment, we're found to be unworthy of God's grace. If that occurs, our spirit would be forever extinguished and we would cease to exist; cease to have knowledge or awareness of anything. It would be as if we never were.

On the other hand, Satan already has eternal life so he must eventually go to the Lake of Fire where his life will not be extinguished but he will forever be quarantined; and thereby punished by being separated forever from God.

The consequence of the original disobedience by Adam and Eve was to corrupt our human state, to corrupt our previously unsullied status. This immediately distanced us from God. He could not condone our presence within His sanctuary if we were unrighteous. The result was that Adam and Eve were expelled from Eden. Once outside God's sanctuary the door was open for all humankind to disregard and disobey God's laws.

God cannot allow us back into His sanctuary whilst we are in a state where we are tainted by sin. To do so would be extremely dangerous for us. God is actually protecting us by preventing us from re-entering His sanctuary without first proving, on an individual basis, that we are righteous.

Were God to allow us back into His sanctuary whilst we are tainted by sin and still have a propensity to choose to break His laws then upon us re-entering and partaking of the Tree of Life we would gain eternal life, but we would be in an ungodly state. This would mean that God could not let our existence end with our mortal death. Instead, He would have to send us to the eternal Lake of Fire to suffer the same fate as Satan. God does not want this for us.

If, as individual humans, we fail to meet God's requirements He prefers to extinguish our lives forever, so that we do not suffer eternally in the Lake of Fire. It's not His wish to harm His people. It is, however, His wish to bring His people back to Him. He wants us to win our battle against unlawfulness (against our carnal ego) and become righteous so that He can extend His grace to us and give us eternal spiritual life.

Don't forget that God expressly forbade Adam and Eve to eat the fruit of the Tree of Knowledge of Good and Evil; warning Adam that he would surely die if he did so (Genesis 2:16-17).

However, Satan persuaded Eve to eat the fruit of that tree. This is when Satan told humanity his first great lie: that humans are immortal and would surely not die if they ate the forbidden fruit. Unfortunately, and surprisingly, this lie about the inherent immortality of the human spirit or soul has persisted in the face of the express words of Genesis 2:16-17 that tell us the opposite. Make no mistake, we will only have eternal life if we are judged by God to be righteous. Otherwise, we will have external non-existence in any form.

Obviously, we are all tainted with the sins of Adam and Eve. Why do I say it is obvious? The answer is fairly simple. Adam and Eve had not had any off-spring before they were expelled from God's sanctuary. Genesis 5:3 tells us that Adam begot a son in his own likeness after his (that is after Adam's) image; meaning in an ungodly, sinful or unrighteous state. Then Adam had other children. All of Adam's children were born outside God's sanctuary. They were born into the world as we know it.

That world, as we have been told, was and still is, Satan's hunting ground. Satan currently has sway over the Earth (1 John 5:19; Ephesians 2:1-3; 1 John 2:15-17). Therefore, Adam's children could not possibly be allowed to return from the carnal, unrighteous ego-driven world that we live in into God's sanctuary, where they would have eternal life, without being or becoming righteous humans and being granted God's grace. Otherwise, Eden would have become full of unrighteous humans with eternal life.

Viewed in this context, the mechanism of original sin was astutely put in place by God to save us from eternal suffering, by ensuring that each of us must achieve either eternal spiritual life with God or go to eternal non-existence where you will not experience anything and will therefore not suffer.

Insight: You have probably gathered from the above that I do not believe that there is eternal damnation in 'Hell' for humans. I rely on Matthew 10:28 and Romans 6:23 for this standpoint. Those who think otherwise appear to rely on Matthew 25:41 and 25:46. However, the proper meaning, in my view to be put on the verses is that the wicked are cast into a fire that annihilates them. They cease to exist. A distinction is drawn in the case of Satan and his demons, who, unlike mortal humans, were created with eternal life. This is precisely why God, in His mercy, created us in a physical state so that we could become righteous and be granted eternal life or be eternally extinguished.

Do not Syncretise (Blend) Your Beliefs...

Having a valid belief system – which to me means believing the Christian scripture – is not about do it yourself ('DIY') or creating your own recipe for universal truth. There is only one universal truth: God's; which is why I say the Roman Catholic Church and mainstream Protestant churches, with their traditions, have syncretised and therefore vitiated the scripture.

Insight: To me only apostolic Christianity – that is the practices and words of the apostles as taught by Jesus – are correct; nothing more and nothing less.

No Goat Yoga with Mantras and Prayer Wheel...

To me, blending, say, Buddhism and Christianity into some user-friendly goat yoga system based on the belief that "God and I have an arrangement, an understanding" is frankly not only wrong but also dangerous. You don't have a private deal with God. We all have the same deal.

When you start talking private deals it's your ego that's doing the talking, once again. Don't get trapped into speaking or believing "... great swelling words of emptiness..." (2 Peter 2:18); do not edify yourself or one another instead of God. You edify yourself when you think that you can have a private, special arrangement with God. Don't delude yourself.

Do not despise the prophecies (1 Thessalonians 5:20) and don't give the prophecies or the scripture your own spin (2 Peter 1:20); because prophecy is not the words of men but the words of holy men of God who spoke as they were moved by the Holy Spirit (1 Peter 1:21).

The above scriptures are plainly saying that you don't have a private deal with God and you must not adulterate the scripture by giving it your own user-friendly, ego-convenient goat yoga mantra mumbling prayer wheel spinning interpretation.

'Enlightenment' or Truth...?

David Hawkins said that Buddha showed the way to enlightenment whereas Jesus came to provide salvation.

So, what is enlightenment?

In Europe, the age of enlightenment refers to a philosophical (that is ego-intellect) movement of the 17th and 18th centuries that promoted science and reason (that is ego-intellect) over what was seen as myth and superstition.

Buddhists would likely see enlightenment as 'satori', the term used by D.T. Suzuki (1870-1966), a Japanese scholar who lived for a time as a Rinzai Zen monk. 'Satori' derives from the Japanese verb 'satoru', meaning 'to know'. The fact is, no one knows what enlightenment means; but it plainly doesn't mean 'truth', and enlightenment won't tell you anything about the purpose or meaning of human life. I know this because it didn't do it for Buddha or David Hawkins.

To me, the concept of 'enlightenment' is totally unenlightening. I prefer to be guided by the scripture which says that you should trust in the Lord with all your heart (not your consciousness, not your intellect, not your reason, but with your heart) and not rely on your own understanding (Proverbs 3:5). We are warned that the way of the fool will always seem right in his own eyes but he who listens to counsel is wise (Proverbs 12:15). We are told not to be wise in our own opinion (Romans 12:16).

The Second-Tier of the MoC...

I've said that I consider David Hawkins' MoC to be only the first tier of what is actually a spiral; and that his MoC is incapable of calibrating the divine because the consciousness of the divine is so infinite as to be all-knowing and all capable.

But what might, say, the second tier of such a MoC look like?

The answer is that we don't know and we don't need to know. What we need to know for this earthly life to be a success is that our prospects for achieving our true purpose are heightened if we can bring forth an ego-less, humble, and contrite teachable heart. If we do that, and only if we do that, can we open the door to acquiring the faith that will lead us on the journey that will result in this earthly life having served its true purpose: to earn us God's grace and salvation so that we pass from this earthly factory bench-testing phase of our existence (our mortal, earthly lives) onto the existence God wants us to have, with all its rewards. We cannot do it by becoming 'enlightened'.

Lose Your Ego and Forget Artificial Intelligence... And Receive Your Heritage...

Much of what is referred to in this section is taken from a free online article from the gospelcoalition.org.

The term artificial intelligence ('AI') was the concept of American computer scientist, John McCarthy. In 1956, he defined it as "getting a computer to do things which, when done by people, are said to involve intelligence". There are different types of AI.

'Narrow AI' is the capability of a machine to perform a limited number and range of intelligent tasks that a human can do. Narrow AI can be programmed to 'learn' in a limited sense but lacks the ability to understand context.

'General AI' refers to the capability of a machine to perform many of the intellectual tasks a human can do, including the ability to understand context and make judgments based on context.

To be artificially intelligent, a machine must have the ability to 'learn'. We now have a science of 'machine learning', that is, getting computers to learn and act like humans. The idea is that these machines will continue to learn and over time will become autonomous.

They learn as a result of being fed data and information in the form of observations and by interaction with the outside world.

All machine learning is AI but not all AI involves machine learning. Machine learning involves training and inference. In the training phase the machine is fed data and information in the form of observations and real-world interactions. The machine examines the data and makes generalisations from the examples provided. The machine then uses algorithms – guidelines that tell a computer how to perform a task – to draw inferences (that is, conclusions based on 'evidence' and 'reasoning').

A typical example of machine learning is teaching computers how to recognise images, such as human faces.

Some AI machines are uncontroversial from the standpoint of scripture. They are performing mundane rote tasks; such as a smart phone giving you a sports result on request. AI machines can also benefit us in areas of health and medical treatment using high-tech procedures such as fMRI or by assisting the physically disabled.

However, there are negative aspects of AI that come onto stark view when one reads books such as *Homo Deus*, by Yuval Harari. I discussed *Homo Deus* in detail in Chapter 8; and I discussed 'machine man' in Chapter 13.

Harari writes of AI taken to the point of replacing humans, or humans 'evolving into' machines. Harari sees this as fine, and even desirable, as he says there is no God and we don't have souls. These sorts of crackpot ideas should be of concern to all of us.

What if Harari's Machine Entities Were in Charge...?

The machine beings envisaged by Harari would have the ethics and morals of those who programmed them; which might be none. They would not be ethically neutral; and they would have intention, free will and the capacity for good or harm.

Given that in, *Homo Deus*, Harari says that God is a myth (p134), humans do not have souls (pp119 and 135), the theory of evolution cannot accept the idea of human souls because a soul has no parts so it cannot possibly result from a step-by-step evolution (p122), what would his machine humans be like? After all, he says the soul belongs in the dustbin of science (p134), that scientists today can do much better than God (p55).

Could we trust these cyborgs to be ethical, to be moral, to be humane? This is a serious concern given that Harari believes human life is no more than a 'dog eat dog existence' and that 'might is right' (*Homo Deus* pp 54, 238, 261); he foresees that we humans will 'disappear' (p53); he sees that these unnatural AI beings would have "divine powers of creation and destruction" (p53); that they "... could love, hate, create and destroy on a much grander scale than us" (p54).

Ask yourself: do the likes of Harari and Raymond Kurzweil (who I mentioned in Chapter 13) reflect what you would like to see for your children's children, for humankind? It amounts to human extermination.

Would These AI Beings Have Hearts...?

What sets humankind apart is that our hearts are not merely physical; they are inherently capable of understanding, knowing, discernment, of being moral and ethical. The human heart is profoundly significant, an integral part and proof of what we are and why we are.

Jesus was part of the Elohim before He cast off His divine being to be born a mortal man, but He always knew of His divine origins (John 8:58) and His earthly purpose (Isaiah 52:13-14; Hebrews 12:2). He was and is the way, the truth and life (John 14:6); the light of the world (John 8:12), conceived by Holy Spirit (Matthew 1:20); led by the Holy Spirit (Luke 4:1).

Jesus focused on men's hearts, not on their intellects; because the intellectually wise who do not know God will be destroyed (Obadiah 8). This is because a mutual antagonism exists between the ego-driven wisdom of the world (Crick, Dawkins, Harari, Sam Harris (*The Moral Landscape*), Raymond Kurzeil, Stephen Hawking, and so on) and the wisdom of God.

This conflict is thrown into stark contrast in the Crucifixion because God works wisely and powerfully in ways that are incomprehensible to ego intellect and ego expectations. Even as Jesus was on the cross the Jews mockingly asked Jesus for a sign that He was the Son of God (Matthew 27:40-43). That's how blind they were.

Jesus in His divine form was and is the Word, the Logos, the God of the Old Testament. He was the King and High Priest Melchizedek of Salem (Genesis 14; Hebrews 7:1-3).

Jesus was concerned with men's hearts and souls: Genesis 6:5-6; Exodus 8:15; 28-29; 31-6; Numbers 15-39; Deuteronomy 4:9, 4:29; 4:39; 6:5-6, 8:2; 10:16; 11:16; 11:18; 28:47, 29:3; 29:17; 30:6; 1 Kings 8:58; 1 Chronicles 29:17; Psalm 28:7; 73-26; 84:3; Proverbs 21:2; Jeremiah 31:33; Ezekiel 11:19 and 26 (a new heart); Matthew 5:8; 6:21; 9:4 and 22: 11:29; 13:15 and 19; 15:18 and 19; 22:37; Mark 2:8; 7:6; 7:21; 12:30 and 33; 16:14; Luke 6:45; 8:12; 16:15; John 7:38, Acts 5:3-4; 7:51; 15:9; Romans 10:9; 1 Corinthians 2:9; Hebrews 8:10; 10:16, Revelation 2:23.

Ego, like pride, will lead to a fall. Even a great Pharaoh is but a passing noise (Jeremiah 46:17). Ego comes at a price to all, regardless of earthly rank; as it did with Herod (Acts 12:19-23). You can measure yourself by your own worldly yardstick but it's a false measure (2 Corinthians 10:12; 11:17). Do not be wise in your own eyes (Proverbs 3:7; 26:5-16).

Conscience Verses Consciousness...

Your heart has a potential purpose that is greater than intellect can ever aspire to (Acts 11:23); something that is beyond the capacity of intellect. For one thing, unlike our intellect, our heart has conscience (Hebrews 10:22). This is also made clear in 1 John 3:20 by the phrase 'if our heart blames us'.

Insight: Consciousness is of far lesser importance than faith and conscience when it comes to your future.

Hence, a New Heart for Mankind...

"I will put My laws in their minds and write them on their hearts. I will be their God and they will be My people" (Hebrews 8:8-10, NIV).

What You Have Learned in This Chapter

- When it comes to spiritual beliefs you have all the resources available to you to find the truth
- Your search for spiritual truth must be a search with the heart and egoless intellect for it to lead to truth
- Faith, which comes from a humble, contrite heart is a far better guide than paltry intellect
- David Hawkins focused on consciousness but consciousness of itself is a dead-end that will not lead to truth

CPSIA information can be obtained
at www.ICGtesting.com
Printed in the USA
BVHW041058280222
630222BV00009B/230